Four Faces of Peru

four faces of
PERU

by

W. BYFORD-JONES

THE TRAVEL BOOK CLUB
121, Charing Cross Road,
London W.C.2

H. 2. 69.

Robert Hale Limited
63 Old Brompton Road
London S.W.7

PRINTED IN GREAT BRITAIN BY
BRISTOL TYPESETTING CO. LTD.
BARTON MANOR - ST. PHILIPS
BRISTOL 2

AUTHOR'S NOTE

PERU, which is the third largest country in South America, is said to have four faces—Lima, the Andes, the Desert and the Peruvian Amazon. It is because of the three great geographical features that the surface of Peru presents such great obstacles to movement about the country from Lima, as also to human habitation. In this book I tell how, after reaching Lima from Bolivia, I went into the desert, over the Andes, and then down the Amazon from the jungle town of Iquitos, across the line which separates civilization from barbarity, to stay with Indian tribes which live a near aboriginal existence.

W.B-J.

For

CYNTHIA LOUISE

CONTENTS

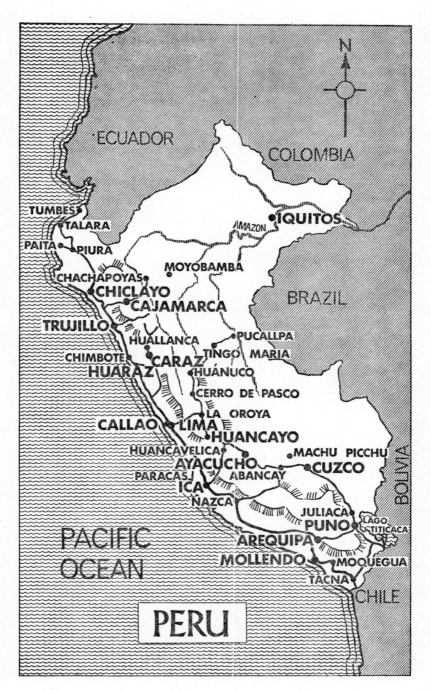

A*

I

A Priceless Heirloom

IT WAS only by crazy chance I went to the extraordinary places I describe in this book. Crazy, perhaps, because the finding of one ear-ring in the folds of an alpaca rug in an hotel lobby caused me to change my carefully worked out travel plans. Instead of going up the Pacific coast of South America to Lima, thence to Colombo, I went to the City of the Kings, as Lima is called, by way of a reckless detour. I eventually crossed the vaguely defined frontier between civilization and barbarity. I penetrated a beautiful and yet terrifying world that is beyond the reach of the Law, a world in which uncounted Indian blow-pipe hunters wage war on a wide variety of wild animals and on each other in the vast jungles and aboriginal forests of the Amazon Basin.

On my way I clambered on to lonely mountain platforms in the high Andes, I plunged into deep canyons gouged out of the grey rock. I saw the undisturbed remains of lost cities of the Incas from which a mighty people had vanished as if into thin air. At least they had left no clues that could be interpreted corroboratively by archaeologists and anthropologists. On my way back I visited the 1,400-mile coastal desert strip of Peru, where, between widely scattered temples, I saw ancient graves from which robbers were still extracting treasure belonging to civilizations earlier even than the Incas.

Representatives of successive civilizations, preserved by the embalming qualities of the sand in areas where no rain falls, squatted on their haunches in attitudes of awareness. As if they still expected promises made to them by their god-emperors to materialise.

On the slopes of nearby mountains there were mysterious lines fifty miles long, drawn as if by giants who gained their perspective from heaven. These, and other strange lines, were keys to a lost logic that might, if properly understood, open up one day a fantastic chapter of prehistory.

When I left England, in the late summer of 1964, foot-loose for South America, I had a vague idea of the route I would take through ten republics. A glance at the map had warned me an open mind was needed. The land surface was cut in two by the mighty Andes which ran for 4,500-miles through the continent to the west at an average height of 13,000-feet. Except in Bolivia, one of the inland countries I was visiting, the mountain chain was 200-miles wide. In Bolivia, where it formed a vast, dreary table-land where a strangely resentful people, and their expectorating animals, existed in remote solitude, the mountains were twice as wide. For good measure there were fifteen peaks up to 22,830 feet with condor-haunted passes from east to west. They were of an average height of 11,000 feet.

Three groups of active volcanoes, at widely spaced intervals, suggested that the devil maintained an active vigil at guard posts along the crest of the Andes. The countryside was further divided by great river systems, in particular by the Amazon, the largest river in the world. The whole of Amazonia sprawls over a million square miles and most of it is covered with jungle and tropical forests in which live thousands of tribes of barbaric Indians who have never seen a white man.

Since a large part of the Amazonian Basin has not yet been explored—many men have ventured into the interior and not returned—the jungle may hide still more lost cities of little known civilizations as well as millions of tribal or nomadic Indians, who know nothing of the civilized world outside. There are parts of Amazonia over which not even aeroplanes venture, because of the danger of being forced to land by engine trouble in places from which there would be no escape. There could even be entirely new animals deep in the jungles of Amazonia; examples of new creatures have indeed been found in and around South America within recent years.

When I reached Chile, after continuous travelling from Brazil to the Argentine via Uruguay and Paraguay, I felt in need of a quiet harbour where I could rest and take stock. Middle Chile is a beautiful and restful land but I could not find happiness there. There were deplorable contrasts of wealth and poverty, between the peons and inquilinos, in their roughly thatched and insanitary mud huts, and the disgustingly rich landowners of the great sprawling haciendas to whom the peasants are tied as if still serfs.

I went on to Arica, Chile's most northern port, which has the best sea bathing in a country only 200 miles wide between the Andes and the Pacific but with a coast 2,800 miles long. I was lucky in a place so small and popular to obtain a quiet room in a pleasant hotel. This was surprising for, apart from its other qualities, Arica was to be my jumping-off place for the entirely unplanned and unexpected journey into which I was to be precipitated by finding the ear-ring. It was just south of the Peruvian, and west of the Bolivian, frontier. It was linked with the legendary birthplace of the Incas by a ten-hour journey into Walt Disney land by a railway, the Arica-La Paz line, which ran both steam trains and diesel cars. Arica was as happy as a town should be which saw so much of the sun and saw no rain, winter or summer. It stood in the lee of the Morro headland and was encircled by sand dunes which reminded one that the hot desert stretched like a saffron ribbon 600 miles all down the coast as far as Copiapo.

One fact puzzled me. There was not the same racial diversity in Chile as in Brazil or Argentina, nor were there so many full-blooded Indians, but Arica seemed to possess a disproportionate share of colour. Of Chile's eight million inhabitants there were in all only 250,000 pure-blooded, indigenous Indians and kindred peoples, and they were mainly confined to the far-away forests between Bio-Bio and the Tolten rivers. Most of the inhabitants of Chile were mestizos, people of an uncertain mixture of blood. The disproportionate number of full-blooded Indians in Arica, some of them unusually wealthy, was due, I learned, to the fact that it had become fashionable as a bathing resort for Bolivians who travelled there by the Arica-La Paz railway. More came each year to enjoy the warm climate, the fine Chilean food, the night clubs and the roulette in the casino. Since Bolivia was landlocked the Andean visitors enjoyed the sea bathing best. The water of Titicaca, the world's highest navigable lake, which Bolivia shares with Peru, was too cold for all but the hardiest bathers.

I had not been in my Arica hotel an hour, and was passing through the hall to persuade a taxi driver to take me to the bathing beach, when Fate steered me in the direction of an old alpaca rug. As I was passing it something glittered and caught my eye. I picked up a crude-looking ear ornament entangled in the wool. It

was a cheap piece of native Indian jewellery, I decided, probably
sold in the Chilean equivalent of Woolworths. I continued to the
door, not thinking it worth handing in at the reception desk. I
might have tossed it into the gutter had I left the hotel. But I
did not. There was no taxi. What was strange, I thought, as I
stood in the porch, sunning myself and rolling the ornament
through my fingers, was that people should waste their time making by hand such amateur-looking ornaments when the West
could mass-produce on their machines more and better things at
a fraction of the price. Then I looked at the ear-ring again and
began to have doubts. In the strong sunlight I could make out
that what I had thought were lines scratched round the edge, were
in fact a succession of tiny figures with big heads, each of them
slightly different. Then I remembered seeing similar designs on
Inca ornaments in the British Museum. Maybe, I began to tell
myself, the ornament was genuinely old despite that the back of it
had been soldered.

There was still no taxi. It was far too hot to walk. I went back
to the reception desk where the clerk was doodling. He did not
hear me ask him to telephone for a cab but when I placed the ear
ornament in a direct line with his eyes he became electrified.

" I found it on the rug over there," I said idly.

The clerk picked up the object as if it were the koh-i-noor.

" You find this?" he said excitedly.

I told him again.

He stared at the object in silence and I swear his eyes glittered.

" The Torezes," he remembered suddenly and lifted the telephone.

As he waited for a reply, his eyes darting here and there, I got
a little sense out of him. The object was not a worthless bit of tin.
It was an antique gold ear-ornament, old as the Incas. It belonged
to an archaeologist, wife of another archaeologist, both Peruvian,
who were on holiday from a mysterious place called Tiahuanaco,
near Titicaca, where they worked with a U.S. team of archaeologists.

" No answer," he muttered at last. He was about to replace the
phone when someone spoke. I could hear a sleepy voice burbling
in the earpiece, a little grieved at being awakened in the middle
of the siesta.

" Mr. Torez," stuttered the clerk, " we've found it. I've got it
here, in my hand."

There was an incoherent reply, like a series of explosions in the earpiece.

"Yes, I *have* it. Found in the hall."

The clerk stared at the telephone. Mr. Torez had rung off in his ear.

"They were sleeping," he explained sheepishly, looking round at the clock. "Very excited." He stared again at the ornament. "It doesn't look much does it?" He jerked his head to the stairs. "They looked all today. Madame cried. They were going to the police. No, it certainly doesn't look much, but that's *it*. They described it perfectly."

Obviously the Torezes had to dress. It was some minutes before they came bounding down into the hall, two stairs at a time. In the meantime the clerk told me about the Torezes. They were young Peruvians, professional archaeologists, and they had spent their honeymoon at the hotel the year before and made a nostalgic return visit a week back.

Mr. Torez won the race to the reception desk. His wife was not far behind him. "Thank God," he said with a Texan accent as he identified the ornament.

"It is *it*?" asked his wife breathlessly.

"It's *it* all right."

I scarcely took any notice of Torez. He was a thickset, brown-faced man with black hair, a cholo or white Indian half-breed, but immaculately dressed. I had eyes only for his wife, a lovely, young, full-blooded Indian who had more latent power than conventional beauty. Her face was oval, with coppery skin and coarse black hair, thick as a mare's mane, dropping on her tawny shoulders. When she brushed unceremoniously past me to snatch the ear ornament from the hands of her husband, I was conscious of the magnetic strength and vitality of her body. I felt her long hair swish through the air close to my cheek as if it were a fly whisk.

She had thrown on a blouse and a skirt and wore no shoes, a simple fact which had an aphrodisiac effect on a man. She had the stark grace and elegance of a wild animal. Perhaps she was no longer a girl, as the clerk had called her. She had begun, since her last visit to her dress-maker to develop a definite maturity, and her dress was nearly new. I noticed that the linen out of which the skirt was cut bore an antique pattern.

Suddenly I was aware that the Torezes and the clerk had turned round to stare at me.

"Thank you," said Mr. Torez, and he introduced himself as Sinchi de la Torez. The girl, or the woman, was "My wife, Peta."

Mrs. Torez stared at me with deep, black, groping eyes. She said nothing with her tongue.

"We are grateful," went on Torez, looking at his wife as if urging her to say something. "It does not look much, but this is *very* valuable. It belongs to my wife's family. It had come down to her through her mother and grandmother from a long line of her people. Naturally she would never have been consoled if she had lost it."

I was glad I had been of some help.

"Let us have coffee," said Torez. He did not wait for me to reply but ordered a pot from the receptionist. "Sit here near the door, it is cool," he said. We all three sat at the table. Mrs. Torez still looked at me and her husband now made his annoyance known.

"You are English, the man says," she asked at last.

"Yes," I admitted. "Just touring South America."

"We have never met English," explained her husband. "We are always with Americans."

"There is not much difference, surely," I said.

"Only the voice," said Mrs. Torez, still fondling the ear ornament. "I like the way English speak." Then she added quickly:

"I have read much about England."

As we drank coffee Torez returned to the ornament.

"It is an heirloom, you see," he said. "It is also historic. It belonged to someone close to the Incas—one of the aculluacuna or Chosen Women. It may even have been given to her by one of the Inca nobles. There are not more than half a dozen pairs of such ear ornaments of this type. Some were found in graves." He took the ornament from his wife's hand and held it in his palm for me to see. "It was cast, by a method archaeologists know as *cire perdue*," he said. "The Peruvian goldsmiths invented it." He pointed to the edges. "You can see it was cast."

I looked at the ornament closely for the first time. I was astonished that casting was known so long ago and said so.

"You are right to be surprised," said Torez approvingly. "Ancient Peruvians pioneered casting. And much else, of course. Does Peru interest you?"

"It certainly does," I said. I was collecting material for a book and I now realized that I had committed the unforgivable crime of forgetting the Incas. The term " Chosen Women ", which Torez had used drifted into my mind again, but in a new context. As a hair gets into the soup, the explanation drifted into my mind that the Chosen Women were a special vintage of hand-picked Inca girls. They were, in fact, chosen by itinerant inspectors who visited the villages of the Inca empire on behalf of the god-emperors to find the most beautiful, the most comely and the most intelligent girls (if such qualities were to be found together). The girls who pleased were taken to Cuzco, the ancient imperial capital of the Incas, and were specially trained and educated. The annual visits must have been like our " Miss Universe " beauty competitions. The girls became concubines to the god-emperor or wives for his brothers or nobles. Of the exact details of the role of the Chosen Women I was not sure but I was pleased to know that much. If, indeed, Mrs. Torez was a direct descendant of one of the Chosen Women that explained her exotic personality and striking bearing.

Mr. Torez was explaining how the Inca goldsmiths cast the ornaments. I only picked up what he said in the middle of the explanation. Apparently a model was made in wax of the desired ornament. The model was then encased in clay, but with a hole at the bottom. The clay was baked, causing the wax to melt and run out of the clay mould. Then pure molten gold was poured into the mould and allowed to cool. When the mould was broken open the casting of the ornament was within.

" Very wasteful," said Torez, " very wasteful. One mould, one ornament. But it made for individuality, something one cannot find today."

We talked about textiles and cloth made by pre Inca and Inca craftsmen and also discovered by tomb robbers in well-preserved graves in the sand. Then I learned that the design of Peta's dress was a copy of the design on a bobbin pattern weave made by the Chosen Women. They had spent their spare time at spindle and loom.

" The Chosen Women," she said, " spent a lot of time making new designs. Some patterns they made have been cleverly reproduced. They have become very fashionable in Lima."

We talked until the receptionist came to me. There was a taxi at the door.

II

Up into the Mountains

REFRESHED BY the rest beside the sea, and instructed by Sinchi and Peta in every phase of the life of the Incas, I left Arica to start my reckless detour. My first stop was to be La Paz, capital of Bolivia, from which I could easily reach Lake Titicaca, passing *en route* through Tiahuanaco.

Peta gave me the address of a man who would explain anything I wanted to know about the old city and another of a woman who would find me a room if I wished to stay. From Guaqui, about ten miles from the ruins, I had only to deliver a letter to be taken by Peta's favourite old boatman to the Islands of the Sun and Moon (El Sol and Coati).

" Go by moonlight if you can," she said. " He will take you if you insist. He has taken me often. It is quite mystical."

The prospect of the journey into the Andes was more exciting because of some of the preparations I had to make. I bought a simple oxygen mask, favoured by people who visited the tin mines, and a supply of oxygen in a plastic bag. I invested in two kinds of tablets which would give me relief when I was attacked by sorochi, or height sickness, and I acquired a thick poncho, a warm coat like an inverted sack with a slit in the top to put one's head through. Sinchi had told me a good deal about the effects of the heights I would encounter even in La Paz. It was the highest capital in the world at an altitude of 12,400 feet, yet the city lay at the foot of a kind of amphitheatre of mountains some 1,500 feet below the surrounding peaks. On reaching high places—I would encounter many of them—I was advised to go to bed for a few hours. If sorochi troubled me then I was to take the tablets. If I went still higher the oxygen mask would help me. At the highest altitudes the cold at night would be intense. I would not be able to keep warm in bed on the Altiplano, or High plateau, on which La Paz and Lake Titicaca were situated, even if I heaped many blankets on to my bed.

The steam train from Arica to La Paz left every Monday after dinner and ran through the night into the morning. The railway was the shortest line to the Pacific from Bolivia. It was built by the Chilean Government under the terms of the Treaty of Friendship of 1904 and was inaugurated in 1913 and handed over to Bolivia in 1928. Its total length was 280 miles, of which 150 were on Bolivian territory and operated by the Bolivian State Railway. To my surprise there were no sleeping cars and the passengers, in two classes, came prepared as if to withstand a siege. The diesel auto car which did the journey quicker cost more.

The train was full when I walked along it after securing a seat by the window. Everyone was fussing about, putting on slippers or stacking luggage or trying to secure an even better seat than the one they had got. Conversation was confined to confidential whispers among small groups of conspirators. Everyone seemed to throw others dark looks. Now and then there was confusion caused by someone impulsively collecting all his baggage from where he had carefully secreted it and struggling with it, to the annoyance of everyone else, to some better seat which had been suddenly evacuated. The evacuee had himself espied what he thought was a still better place. The passengers in the lower class were more direct and open, and the odour of sour, blistered feet bared to the air commingled with the spicy smell of food. This was devoured with unaffected pleasure and as if time was against the eaters.

The Titicaca Indians huddled together as if for protection. They looked sad and suspicious, utterly out of place in a mechanically propelled world. One carriage was unlit, except by the reflection of the platform lights and all I could see were white teeth and white eyeballs. The brown skins and the remote shoe-button-like pupils melted into the dark. The Indian women (70 per cent of Bolivia's population are Indian) kept together and kept apart from the Chola women. They could be distinguished by their hats which each wore as an emblem, winter and summer, throughout their lives, to establish ethnical origin. The Indian women wore brown or grey bowlers of the kind now fashionable among young bloods in London. The Cholas boasted white top hats made of

ripolined straw. The two groups also spoke different languages
and at times seemed to try to shout each other down. The
Indians spoke either Aymara or Quechua, according to the area
from which they came, while the Mestizos spoke Spanish with an
admixture of Indian words.

Back in my seat I found everyone had settled down and I was
able to take stock of the passengers in turn. Only one was a European. He had no book, or newspaper to give me a clue as to his
language or nationality, but his features and his build suggested
he was Flemish. He picked up my glance and returned it and we
both smiled at the same time, part apologetically and part in
salutation.

" English?" asked the man, betraying a Welsh accent.

" Do I give myself away?"

" Oh, I don't know," smiled the man. " I noticed that map
of the Central Andes with English legends."

" You're not English?"

" Welsh," he said. " I live in Chile but I can't deny myself the
mountains. This is the best way to see them, from Arica. I'm on
holiday from the sheep farm, indulging my one real hobby, mountain railways."

I had travelled all over the world, but I had never felt so
' foreign ' as on that train, at least not until the Welshman mentioned the sheepfarm. Then I was suddenly at home, at least in a
valley where I most like to be, Cwn Einion, with its trout streams,
its few scattered sheepfarms and its enclosing mountains dotted
with animated bundles of wool.

" I have a cottage there," I said. " Thank you for mentioning
it. I can so easily evoke its beauty. The sounds of a roaring river,
the falls, the bleat of sheep."

In a moment the Welshman had somehow changed places with
the man next to me. I could feel the warmth of a vibrant nostalgia.
We were together and yet far away.

" When did you leave Wales?" I asked pursuing the topic that
gave him most pleasure.

" I never left Wales," he said.

I smiled, a little confused. " You mean?"

" No. I've never been to Wales," he said, " though I feel I
know it intimately. My grandfather came to Chile from Wales to
work in one of the pioneer regions. But I still say I'm Welsh. He
should have gone with the Welsh Mayflower to Argentina but he

missed the boat. Quite a number of Welsh people came to take up sheep rearing in Atlantic Chile. My father went back. Fought in the first World War. I've never been able to manage it. I've just read *How Green is my Valley*. It brought it all back. Oh, I'll go one day. If it weren't for the rain, I'd stay."

The train ran due east at an almost uniform distance from the Peruvian frontier. When we were passing near the Lluta valley the Welshman showed me pictures he had taken of it on an earlier visit. He talked evocatively as only a Welshman could. It seemed strange to me that his family had kept a trace of the dialect.

Suddenly, he paused. "Listen," he said with Gaelic drama. "This is where my pulsebeat rises. I feel I am in the Welsh mountains." There was a bump and a shout. The train shuddered. We had reached kilo 70. The train began to climb dramatically, so I was told, at about 8,000 feet in half an hour. When the line was racked for thirty miles the Welshman sat silent, listening, as if to some Beethoven symphony. After this had ended he remained quiet. We passed through a tunnel cut beneath the Andean mountains.

The train reached the Altiplano, of which I had heard so much from Peta, a few miles beyond Pupuios station. Already I was feeling tired and a little giddy. The altitude was 13,577 feet. My friend must have detected the signs of discomfort in my face. He said by day I should fix my eyes on snow-capped heights ahead, first on the Huaylas and later on the Tacora, Sajama and Putre. The distant heights prevented one thinking one was as high as one was. This did not help me. I felt a crisis approaching as we travelled at a funeral pace between General Lagos (14,000 feet) and the Bolivian frontier station of Visviri. How I gulped tablets without water I shall never know.

The sheep farmer was telling me how Chile had built the railway to La Paz as a consolation prize to Bolivia when it withdrew its support from Peru in the 1879-83 war against Chile. The war had been a struggle for possession of the Atacana desert and its valuable nitrate fields, but I was unable to learn further details. A man came skipping down the gangway calling out something in Quechua.

"What's wrong?" I asked. "He seems excited."

"Half breeds get excited about nothing," he said. He went on to talk about railways and war. "Bolivia is the unluckiest country

in South America," he said. "It's lost some of the best of its
territory in wars with its neighbours. It's a wonder it hasn't lost
all its most valuable asset, the tin mines. When the Argentine
pinched some of the Chaco, a great lowland covered with scrub
forest and grassy savannah, Bolivia got another consolation prize
of a railway. Still another when Brazil annexed Acre at the beginning of the century."

People in this part of South America were inordinately proud
of their railways. This was obvious in the way my fellow passenger regarded railway officials. The train stopped at an unscheduled
halt, and remained there without any apparent reason for an un-
conscionable time. The passengers did not grumble. Sometimes
they did not even bother to look out of the carriage windows or
ask questions of the officials to find out why the train had stopped.

It was not until the train had reached Viacha, the junction of
several lines that the Welsh sheep farmer left. I must confess to
bathing joyously in the silence that followed. He had several other
train journeys in mind, to Guaqui and Huanchaca in particular,
and he promised to write to me and tell me how he fared. The
train began to start again after a lengthy pause and then stopped
and backed again into the station.

The passengers now began to talk animatedly in their Indian
dialects. It was then that I missed my companion. I heard the
name Oruro mentioned as if it had been the scene of some
disaster. People walked excitedly through the carriage, dropping
odd words that had the effect of hand grenades among those who
understood them. I knew some Spanish and asked several people
to enlighten me. I was rewarded only by shrugs and expressions of
bewilderment. Oruro was a mining town. I knew that the Bolivian
miners tried to dominate the political life of the country because
they produced three-quarters of the country's revenue. I wondered
what they had done now. They had from time to time held nation-
wide strikes and come into violent conflict with the military and
the police. I recalled that revolutions and *coups d'état* were almost
part of public life in Bolivia. They gave the ordinary man an
opportunity to get in some target practice with the revolver or the
rifle he habitually kept in the cupboard or under the bed.

People began to leave the train and walk along the platform to
enjoy the cool morning air and to shake off the fatigue of night
travel, or so I thought. I sat in my tight corner looking out on
Bolivia, now and then consulting my map and wondering why

Bolivia did not look a prosperous country in view of its production of tin, copper, silver, wolfram and gold. It looked what it was, one of the poorest and least literate countries in South America. It was, indeed, so poor that up to 1960 the U.S. had had to support it with some 130,000,000 dollars in loans and grants. Up to the 1952 revolution, led by Paz Estenssoro, who became President of the country, the tin mines had produced the ore equivalent of 300,000 tons of tin a year to provide the country's means to live and trade. Soon after the revolution when Paz Estenssoro had succeeded in his ambition, the output of tin had fallen to about 18,000 tons of tin a year. The formerly profitable tin mines began to lose a million dollars a month. The United States made still more loans and grants. Bolivia obtained more United States' aid per capita than any other country in Latin America. Per capita income, despite the high wages of the tin miners, was then only about £45 a year.

In February, 1964, Paz was again nominated as the Presidency candidate despite that he had promised Lechin, his deputy, that he would succeed to the office of President that year. According to the constitution, before Paz thoughtfully altered it, he could not succeed again to the Presidency. He appointed a new deputy, Lechin was rejected. Naturally the enmity between Paz and Lechin became intensely bitter. Lechin did not stand in the election, which he declared illegal. He called on his own supporters to return blank papers.

Since only Paz Estenssoro stood for office he had easily been elected in May, 1964. Lechin had said he would have opposed him but he was prevented from doing so. The new party Lechin had formed, and which sponsored his candidature, was prohibited for trumped up reasons. Lechin ordered the members of the union of which he was president not to vote but this did not prevent Paz Estenssoro from achieving a valid victory. It was 'proved' that the election had been 'properly conducted' and that seventy per cent of the electorate had polled. Paz took office for a third term after the law preventing such a succession had been altered.

The new President was met on all sides with opposition from Lechin and the miners in his union. The United States again came to the rescue of the sluggish economy with loans.

One outbreak of trouble had followed another and no one knew when the country was going up in flames again. There had been 179 revolutions and *coups d'état* in Bolivia in the past century.

Though I did not know it at the time the 180th had broken out. That was why my train was held up. That was why the passengers left it to talk in excited groups all along the platform.

The fact was President Paz Estenssoro was nearing the end of his political career. He was for the time directing operations from no one knew where. Soon he was to hand over his office to a military junta, of the kind which flourished like evil weeds from time to time all over South America, and to flee for his life to Peru.

An official who spoke with an American accent, and who walked the length of the nearly empty train looking for something or somebody, advised me to remain in the train and not to take my luggage out of it as the others had done.

"The train will soon leave for La Paz," he said. "La Paz will be safer. They are used to revolutions there. They know how to handle them."

I did as I was told and I was thankful for it. When the announcement was made that the train was departing the passengers stampeded like a horde of wild cattle on the Pampas in an effort to get back into their seats.

III

Country of Contrasts

BOLIVIA IS a land divided against itself, not only politically and socially, but ethnically and geographically. On the one hand there is a primitive Indian population that seems permanently impoverished. On the other a small, shrewd, sometimes ruthless, commercial minority which flaunts its white ancestry, or what it declares to be white. Some 70 per cent of the 3,800,000 population is illiterate and this in itself engenders an air of frustration. The literate hate the illiterate. The dark-skinned Indians dislike the acquisitive overlords of Spanish origin. The poor resent the rich. The rich exploit the poor.

The country itself is separated into hostile geographical compartments. A barrier of mountains separates the hinterland from the Pacific and this hinterland is sub-divided by another range of mountains into the high, bitter and barren Altiplano (on which the Spanish conquerors built the political capital, La Paz, in 1548), and the semi-tropical lowland. The lowland is again divided into dense tropical forest and open plains. Added to all this are the climatic differences. The Altiplano is freezing cold. The lowlands are fiercely hot.

The most remarkable feature of the country is that most Bolivians prefer to live in the inhospitable wilderness of the Altiplano. In all 75 per cent of the population live at an altitude above 10,000 feet in a tenth of the country's area. Some of the rich people even prefer to take their holidays in Lhasa, a ski resort, which stands at 16,500 feet, at which height I could not summon up the energy to put one foot before another. In general the people seem as grim as their lunar landscape. They are genuinely at home in the barren frigidity of the gale-swept solitudes. They are not affected by the monotony of the flat land or the absence of trees. They dare not, however, trust themselves in the low-lands.

The Altiplano, original home of the potato, of which there are 150 local varieties, is also the home of three animals strange to the European, the vicuna, the llama and the alpaca. These can be found in small herds where there is grass. The haughty llama is also to be seen in La Paz and in the mineral towns of the Alti-plano, as a beast of burden and in herds in the main streets. Enemy of the llama foals is the condor, the biggest bird in the world, that is to be seen flying over the plateau. The bird breeds on the peaks around this remarkable geographical feature at heights of about 15,000 feet. In contrast, and the country is full of contrasts, the ostrich is to be found on the sparsely populated lowland tropics which are drained ultimately by the Madeira, a tributary of the Amazon. The country has some 200,000 square miles of Amazonian forests.

Bolivia is the home of superlatives. It has the highest capital in the world. The highest navigable lake. It has the highest ski-lift (18,300 feet). The highest ski run. It has the highest golf course—at Mallasilla. It has the highest airport, El Alto, where there is also a station at which my train stopped.

While the train waits at El Alto it is possible to obtain the most wonderful view of mountains over 20,000 feet, snow capped against the blue sky, and to continue to view an ever changing landscape as the train descends into La Paz. The country comes second only in regard to the altitude of its railways. Highest in Bolivia is General Lagos 13,930 feet, but this is dwarfed by the Lima-Oroya-Huancayo railway which reaches its greatest altitude of 15,800 feet inside a tunnel between Ticlio and Galera.

I found La Paz situated in the most unlikely place for a capital city. Its altitude was 12,400 feet and yet it lay at the base of, and was sheltered by, a solid amphitheatre of mountains. As I des-cended to the foot of this natural refuge from the Altiplano gales on the western edge of the canyon, I was over-awed by the Illampa (21,580 feet), the Illamani (21,515 feet) and the Huayna Potosi (20,200 feet). The Altiplano, a veritable planet riding above the world, loses some of the drama of its 13,000 feet alti-tude by comparison, though it regains it in the more startling corners of its 40,000 square miles.

My first contact in La Paz was with a dark Indian girl in her teens who had a doll-like, year-old baby wrapped in a bright, striped shawl. She also had another child, aged three, tugging at her multiple polleras, or skirts, each of them of a different colour. I bought a comb from her for she would not take my peso boliviano as a gift. She had probably learned her lesson not to take money from men in a now discarded profession. A pretty stewardess of the Lloyd Aero Boliviano, with whom I had travelled from El Alto, told me she had helped the girl before when she was having her first child. She had apparently been launched into prostitution by her elder sister who had collected two babies in twenty months.

The sun was hot and brilliant but the peasant women continued to wear their shawls, their polleras and their narrow-brimmed black or brown bowler hats.

Simchi Torez had told me that when he stayed in La Paz there was no fire engine, or fire brigade, in the city, the only capital in the world to be without fire-fighting facilities. The reason, he said, was that the atmosphere in La Paz was so deficient in oxygen there was no risk of fire breaking out accidentally.

I did not like the look of the crowds in the streets. I got a taxi and told the Indian driver to take me quickly round the city centre so that I could orientate myself and then drive me to the Sucre Palace or the Copacabana Hotel, whichever came first. The city was tense as a high powered electric cable so I sat well back in the shadows of the tonneau as we sped through the streets. No one paused for a moment to look in a window or to talk to a fellow pedestrian. People's faces were grim. They gave each other furtive and distrustful looks. In the Alameda, the Plazas Venezuela and de Estudiante, usually paced by animated crowds, University students among them, at this time of the day, were as unfrequented as if it were past midnight. People hurried home as if a storm was threatened, a cloud might burst at any moment. The tragedy of a divided, cowering city was revealed by a comic incident. As we waited in the comparative quiet of a square for the traffic lights to change, the gases of the exhaust pipe of a highly charged car back-fired with the startling sound of a mortar bomb to reverberate all round the buildings. In a moment scores of lurking people, civilians as well as policemen and soldiers, suddenly materialized like so many ghosts at midnight. There were staring faces everywhere, in windows, through doorways, round corners and behind walls. Everyone was armed and ready to fire. It seemed to me that the entire population of La Paz was lying doggo waiting for some such signal to begin the revolution in real earnest. The police all wore respirators at the ready round their necks as if they expected an attack of tear gas.

The driver laughed and drove off as the signal changed. He had told me he was born, and had lived all his life, in the Indian quarters on the higher terraces and was so used to the lawlessness of the Avenida Buenos Aires, " the most notorious street in all Bolivia " that a mere revolution held no terror for him.

" There's been one clash already today," he said, as he slowed down at my hotel. " They weren't quite ready and it died down but this can't go on for long. They're spoiling for a fight. I don't mind, because it's good for trade. When hell breaks loose the old ones will be after a cab to get away."

The porter who took me and my baggage to a front room said conversationally that he thought there was going to be a revolution after all. He spoke in a tone his English counterpart might have used to convey the fear that rain was threatened. He knew what revolution was. He could remember the bloody affray in 1946. Then the President was shot and hanged from a lamp-post outside his own palace. Now, he complained, they could not find the President. Then there was the revolution in 1952. It had been high time there was another. People had been expecting one for some time. La Paz was the capital of the most turbulent country in the world. The trouble with Bolivia, said the porter, was that the men all had revolvers, rifles or even sten guns which they kept wrapped in oiled cloth ready for the fray. Some of them would be out of practice and would not be able to shoot straight. It was terrible that firearms were so plentiful.

" Have you a gun?" I asked as I tipped him.

" Two," he smiled. " I have my father's now. He killed in last revolution."

The head porter was curious to know why an Englishman had come from the other side of the world to this remote city in the very heart of the revolution season. He asked me surreptitiously if he could help me, as if he thought I was a Scarlet Pimpernel come to rescue some eminent person from the jaws of death. It speaks volumes for the race of head porters that he did not bat an eyelid when I told him I was not interested in the revolution, only in a strange group of people who lived thousands of years ago in isolation and mystery at nearby Tiahuanaco.

He could have said quite truthfully that if ruins were all I wanted I need not leave the city because there would be plenty when the revolution got underway. Instead, speaking with the detached concern of a Jeeves, as if a mere revolution was just one of the irritating concerns of a normal day, he suggested I should lose no time in visiting the nearby National Museum in Calle Don Bosco. Though it is built in the Tiahuanaco style, the museum gave me no clue to the fact that it was going to initiate me into as profound a mystery concerning a lost civilization as can be found in history.

Within a few minutes of being admitted by a weary curator I was lost to the world. Forces were quickly mobilizing in the streets round the museum when I entered it but they could have rocketed with gunfire in the three hours I was inside and I would not have known about it. When the curator suddenly appeared in the half shadows beside me as I was examining a collection of fabulous gold plate and vessels which the ancient people had made I nearly jumped out of my skin, not that he looked very much like a member of the cult in his official uniform.

"It's time to close," said the man. "I know how time flies when you start going into Tiahuanaco. Even now I lose myself for hours when I'm on my own."

I told him there was only one greater mystery in the world than how Tiahuanaco became abandoned without trace. That was why anyone ever settled on such a wild, isolated site, a glacial eyrie, if ever there was one.

"There isn't a mystery like it, anywhere," he agreed. "How on earth could they have quarried the vast slabs of rock and the huge monoliths and moved them without any draught animals to the site? And who taught them to make such wonderful statuary, gold goblets and drinking vessels? It is as if they just happened, were born fully developed, as great artists, sculptors, builders, and then vanished again. They were developed out of their time. Then darkness came after them."

My mind was full of what I had read about this mysterious cult 13,234 feet up in the icy cold of the barren Altiplano, this so called "Golden city" of pre Inca days near to the shores of Titicaca, the highest navigable lake in the world. I was overcome by the glamour and mystery of it all, impatient to get out of La Paz and go there.

As we walked to the door the curator, forgetting that he wanted to be home before the revolution started, turned to tell me that there were many theories about Tiahuanaco. He told me of this and that professor who thought it had been the centre of a great cult connected with sun worship, or that it was the centre of a Megalithic empire, or that it was the birthplace of America, or, indeed, of the world.

The Altiplano, he said, was thought by some experts to have been originally an island which for centuries was sunken in the Pacific but which, as a result of some cataclysmic force, was raised as an entity, together with the mighty Andes, to its present high altitude.

" It has such moods," he said, wrinkling his brow. " One day you'll go there with a party and it will be brilliantly light and sunny and you will wonder why other people did not follow the early inhabitants and continue to live there. Then, on another, at the same time of the year, it will be dark and dismal in between the lonely mountains and you'll feel the threat of something, not weather, if you follow me, but like a threat from above, and you'll be glad to get out of it. It can't be more desolate, more icy or more isolated on the moon. Some visitors tell me that when there are earth tremors they fear that the Altiplano will subside to the bottom of the sea and be lost again to the world."

I wanted to do nothing more than go there, to absorb its strange atmosphere, of which the curator had spoken, to examine the massive relics that the civilization had left behind to baffle posterity. Sinchi and Peta had told me that Tiahuanaco was linked with the lost continents of Atlantis and Mu, even with the mysterious Biblical Ophir, and the curator had corroborated what else they had said. Philologists had told the official, and he showed me the statement in official guides, that the Aymara language spoken by the Indians on the Altiplano was the first speech spoken by man, the language which Adam and Eve spoke in Eden. Tiahuanaco, was, in fact, the Garden of Eden, he said, the birthplace of man, the place where the whole business of living began. I saw documents which certified that archaeological remains that had been recently found in Peru indicated that man had lived on the Altiplano for over 10,000 years. Dr. Romero Mattos Mendreta, the well known professor of archaeology at the National Central University of Huancayo, whom the curator had met had gone further. He had claimed publicly that crude stone weapons, llama bones and domestic utensils found during excavations in the district of Ondores, proved that people had been living in the Andes

12,000 years ago. Peruvian man, associated with the Andes and the Altiplano, was by far the oldest man in America—subsequent remains, for which searches were being made, might prove that he was the oldest in the world.

When I left the museum I felt that I was coming out of a trance, that the curator had cast a spell over me and not quite released me from it. My departure from La Paz next morning was partly an escape from a revolution and partly an adventure into a strange world lost in the mists of antiquity.

I left by taxi for the station early through streets mainly occupied by security forces who had erected barricades. Obviously I am a prodigious collector of revolutions. One in Spain, another in Bulgaria, a third in Cyprus and a fourth in Greece had fully initiated me into the fraternity which specialized in revolution collecting. I had been admitted to exclusive circles because I could converse authoritatively on these bloody experiences with people who exchange recollections with the fervour little boys used to swop cigarette cards in the thirties. The trouble was, and I had so often been made to feel it by more experienced collectors, I lacked even a single South American revolution just as the little boys sometimes lacked a card which spoiled a set. The revolution and *coup d'état* were a frequent event in the republics. They were almost part of normal government in some countries. They certainly saved the fag of holding elections. I had seen such events only in American films and they always made revolutions look like sporting events in which ceremonially clad generals shouted and waved their sabres from the backs of rearing steeds. I had, to be truthful, looked forward to at least one revolution. My travel agent had not exactly guaranteed one but he had gone so far as to say I was almost certain to run into one since I was visiting so many South American republics. Now a revolution was about to begin, had in fact begun in some parts of the country, and I was going away to look into the facts of a civilization that had died so many centuries ago and left no trace.

We had not gone very far before two Bolivians of middle age with bundles held us up by the simple expedient of standing in our way. When one spoke to the driver I noticed that there suddenly appeared in one cheek a round bulge, very much like the lump in the cheek of a squirrel. Then I noticed that after he had spoken the lump disappeared and he began to chew with a short, sharp, regular motion. The driver, who had been chewing as he listened to what they said, began to answer them and a big lump came in one of his cheeks.

I remembered vaguely that people in the train, the taxi driver, the hall porter, the curator and others I had met the day before had also been chewing, though I could not recall seeing the bulges in the cheek. I made it clear to the driver that I wanted him to give the couple a lift, at least as far as the station. He argued but gave way. As the two Bolivians sat on the opposite seat to mine in the cab the squirrel-like bulges were most apparent. The two smiled lamely, knowing they could not speak my language. When they thought they had given me the appropriate quota of grateful smiles for the short distance they were to travel they became solemn again. The bulges vanished and the chewing began again. Now Bolivians will not smile if they can help it. I think they would rather cry. But smiling is not a natural state in a landscape so bleak and an atmosphere so icy. I think it would cause pain if smiling was kept up for too long. Continual chewing saves them having to smile at anyone since it is manifestly impossible to smile and chew at the same time.

All the inhabitants of this bleak Altiplano chew continually. They favour not gum, but a tea-like leaf called coca (*Erythroxylon coca*), which grows in jungle and forest. The coca is rich in cocain which is released slowly as it is chewed—quicker, if lime is added. The addicts carry a gourd of lime made from calcined shells and dip into it from time to time a stick which they suck. Purpose of chewing the coca is to increase the powers of endurance of the peasants on this inhospitable plateau, to relieve their hunger and appease their thirst. How much is consumed may be judged from the fact that 32,000 tons of coca leaves are harvested annually. Though the leaves produce between 85 and 150 tons of cocaine only 1.3 tons are used medically. The rest is chewed with the result that addicts become irresolute and dissolute.

I noticed on the rest of the way that Bolivians have a purely nationalistic way of chewing. Not in a semi-circular motion like that other human ruminant, the G.I., but in a straight up and down motion rather like, but with far shorter chews, the Arabs south of the Red Sea who are partial to khat leaves.

IV

Mists of Antiquity

A FERVENT prayer to the Indian Household God, Ekeko—he looks like an inebriated Santa Claus—for I survived the train journey from La Paz without beginning to chew my cud. It was necessary to fight my way out of the compartment. The windows, firmly shut the entire way against the cold wind, had become covered with steam. No one was able even to look out at a station at which we stopped unless someone took the trouble to wipe a porthole on the glass. I was glad that all the passengers chewed like so many contented Jerseys in a meadow because that meant they did not smoke. If they had smoked I would have been asphyxiated.

Leaping out on to the icy platform I jumped about to get circulation moving. The energy made me breathe deeply and I noticed that the air was fresh and clear, as I have before now only experienced it while ski-ing in Switzerland. The air stung my air passages and bit into the lobes of my ears and soon I felt my fingers tingling. To add to this I felt the discomfort of height sickness.

On three sides of where I was, in a typical Tiahuanaco landscape, were the white mountains, so called because they are perpetually snow-bound, and on the fourth side of me I sensed the damp, clammy hand of Titicaca, twelve miles to the rear. The train vanished at the end of the platform in the direction of Guaqui and I looked round forlornly on a world which had not been made for me, or for anyone else so far as I could see. The landscape was so repelling as I approached the sacred site that I might have landed on the moon by rocket and set about a reconnaissance to see if life there existed. There were no trees or high shrubs or very much grass and the wind whistled with the eloquence of a B.B.C. drama department gale across the desolate

B

tundra, causing bits of paper, the first sign of human presence, to scud at my heels like terrified kittens.

I had come to Tiahuanaco as to a holy shrine, with bated breath almost, intimidated by an overstrung curator and I felt that I was beholding one of the great enigmas of history, seeing the place where people had built a city almost at the beginning of time. Pulling my poncho around me I resolved to be brave. There was no other train that day so there was no alternative but to seek lodgings with the woman whose name Peta had given me.

At the entrance to the devastated area, a landscape of mystery if ever I saw one, I wondered how human beings at any stage of the history of the world could have been so insensible to cold and to a harsh and inhuman environment as to have chosen this desolate, windswept and treeless desert on which to build a city. I wondered, too, why they had chosen so outlandish a place at the top of the world. I felt that the disciples of the cult, or agents of the empire who were responsible must have searched the Andes for years before they found this hideously isolated site. Obviously the builders were not looking for human comfort or convenience. By descending the mountains they could have found an unfrequented site with all the privacy anyone could have desired in a semi-tropical area. It was strange, since water is essential to life as to most rituals, barbaric or not, that the builders did not choose to build near to the lake, on which they would also have been able to organize transport by Balsas—primitive boats, made out of reeds that grow in the water. I even wondered, when I felt the worst of the cold, if maybe Tiahuanaco had been the centre for some forbidden cult, the rites of which would not bear scrutiny even by primitive peoples. Or that it had been the centre of an invisible empire, like the Ku Klux Klan, and had drawn its secret adherents from respectable walks of life in unsuspecting societies between the mountains and the coast. How, otherwise, would anyone have built a city in this place or have persuaded people to live there or visit it? These mysteries faded into insignificance beside a still greater one. The huge buildings of great stone blocks seemed to have been created out of nothing. There is no quarry nearby from which the stone could have been obtained. No great stone blocks such as are here erected have been found lying about on the ground anywhere near Tiahuanaco. Even if there was a quarry a few miles away the question would have remained how did these primitive people without any knowledge of the wheel and without any animals bigger than the llama have transported the material in such monolithic hunks?

At the entrance to the ruins there is a miraculously surviving ten-foot-high monolithic gateway, known as Gateway of the Sun, with the figure of a weeping god, which is the recurrent motif of Tiahuanacan culture, set right in the middle at the top of a massive frieze. The purpose of the gate had vanished with the disappearance of high walls which were attached to it, and which had deeply enclosed this mysterious city. I tried to imagine what it was like in far-off days when this twelve-ton gate, carved out of a single block of andesite, was the guarded access to the city and when one had to knock upon it with one's staff and wait to be scrutinized and questioned and probably rejected. As the hot sun came out to temper the cold wind I paused to examine the gate. The frieze, which cracked obliquely when it fell earlier, comprised four distinct horizontal compartments over the rectangular gateway. The stone on which it is carved weighed about three tons and yet it had been somehow hoisted ten feet on to columns of similar weight. Scrutinizing the frieze I saw some fifty small, rectangular figures all running towards the god in the centre. I was astonished by their minute detail and finical artistry and they reminded me of the tiny figures on Peta's ear ornament. In the years I earned my living as a black and white artist I recalled how, in moments of indecision, I had doodled and drawn lots of similar little figures, crude and yet animated, unanatomical and yet bursting with life. The designs in the frieze are repeated time and time again on all ceramics, textiles and pottery, made by the same people. The heat of the sun radiating from the head of the god is as familiar as the condor, puma and snake heads found elsewhere. Each of the runners carry staffs in their hands. Nearby are some twenty-five pillar-like statues over twenty feet tall, also containing the symbol of the weeping god. There are many other strange objects, including the Acapana, a terraced pyramid about 50 feet high and about 700 feet on each side. The pyramid, over 13,000 feet above sea level, surrounded by icy cold, inevitably reminds the traveller of Egypt with its desert heat. It is absurd, however, as one magazine did, to liken the pyramid with the Step pyramid of Sakkara overlooking the city of Memphis and built by Imhotep in the third dynasty of Egypt. Nearby there are the remains of a reservoir, a canal and underground compartments. There are also remnants of strongly built dwellings. One of the more impressive ruins is of an assembly area, about 500 feet square, marked out by upright columns which might once have supported a continuous wall. Further away from the gateway are remains of palaces. Scattered about, some lying and some standing, there are basalt blocks, some of them trimmed carefully, and fitted together, and weighing between fifty and a hundred tons. They reveal no marks of having been hauled over uneven land. Some of the most famous remains are the gargantuan human statuary, figures with frightening features, great portholes for eyes, flat noses, tombstone teeth, faces deeply lined. The best statue was found by the American Peruvianist, Wendell C. Bennett, who has written interesting books in America. This twenty-one foot tall sandstone figure of fear was presented to the Bolivian capital.

Within an hour in the bleak landscape, especially if undisturbed by the Indian women and their resentful menfolk, who wander about the wilderness looking for sparse pasture, one becomes lost to the world. Within the delimiting columns I was safely in the arms of the remote past, entirely cut off from the twentieth century. It seemed absurd to think that I had been brought there by one of the remarkable railways of the Andes, still more absurd that I had come from far-off Britain by jet plane. I could easily fool myself I was back in the days of horse and sail. Electricity and television in this milieu seemed unlikely miracles. The Indians were like the survivors of a shipwreck on an unchartered island.

I had over the years visited many ancient, ruined cities but I was never quite so bewildered as by Tiahuanaco. I had not long before visited Cyrene on the North African coast with a charming woman who was a regular contributor to *Punch*. We had found the ruins enclosed by an efficient wall. The equally efficient gate was locked for the night. We were leaving early next morning and could not deny ourselves the pleasure of seeing Cyrene again, especially by the light of a full moon. We had recklessly climbed over the high gate and down the other side but the lady's husband with more respect for regulations, stayed on the correct side, and uttered his protests as he settled down to wait our return. We found, as we wandered through Cyrene, that the light of the full moon magically restored the city to architectural perfection. No longer were there any ruins. The broken columns, the shattered terraces, the splintered pavements and the tumble-down palaces were just as the builders had left them before Time had begun to wreak havoc upon them. Neither of us, in the silver silence of that magical night, would have been surprised to meet Romans in their togas strolling leisurely through the streets, or to hear laughter filtering through the open doorways. We wandered about delighted as two children, declaiming from the forum and pronouncing stray lines of Greek drama from the amphitheatre. The moon even filled the half-empty Roman bath and repaired the stone steps that led down into the water. I fear I may have bathed but for the fact that my companion's husband had overcome his distaste of trespassing and come over the gate to meet us. I felt then, as I have felt since, that the eroding masonry for a brief insane interval actually had been healed by the magic of the moon and we saw Cyrene as it had been so long ago. I remembered all this in Tiahuanaco, but try as I would I could not make this far more mysterious place come to life. It remained dead, enigmatic and cold as ice at a height that can scarcely be exceeded by the highest peaks in Switzerland.

One of the first people to describe Tiahuanaco was Pedro de Cieza de Leon, about whose views on the Incas Harriet de Onis wrote in 1958. He said that this mysterious place in western Bolivia was famous for its great buildings which, without question, were a remarkable thing to behold:

Near the main dwellings there is a man-made hill, built on great stone foundations. Beyond this hill there are two stone idols of human shape, the features of which are beautifully carved so that they seem to be the work of great masters or artists. They are so big that they seem giants. They wear long robes, different from the attire of the natives of these provinces. They seem to have an ornament on their heads. Nearby, there is another building, whose age is baffling. The people who lived here could not write and for this reason no one knows who built these great strongholds or how long ago. Some of the stones are very worn but others are so large that one wonders how human hands could have brought them to where they stand. They are carved in different ways. Some of the stones are in the form of human bodies, and these must have been the idols. Along the walls there are many underground hollows and cavities. Further to the west there are other greater antiquities, many large gates with jambs, thresholds and door all of a single stone. What struck me most when I was observing and setting down these things was that from these huge gateways other still larger stones project on which they were set, some of which must have been thirty feet wide, fifteen or more long, and six feet thick, and this and the door, jamb, and threshold were also one single stone. I cannot fathom what kind of instruments, or tools, were used to work them, for it is obvious that before these huge stones were dressed and brought to perfection they must have been much larger. One can see that these buildings were never completed, for all there is of them are gateways and other stones of incredible size. Some of them were prepared to go into a building. One great stone idol, which these people probably worshipped, stands a short distance away in a small recess. It is even said that beside this idol a quantity of gold was found. Round the shrine there were a number of other stones, large and small, dressed and carved like those already mentioned. In conclusion I would say that I would consider this place to be the oldest antiquity in all Peru. I have heard Indians say that the Incas built their great edifices of Cuzco along the lines of the wall to be seen in this place. They go even further. They say that the first Incas talked of setting up their court and capital here. Another strange thing is that there are neither quarries nor rocks in this region. I asked the natives in the presence of Juan Varagas (who holds an *encomieda* over them) if these buildings had been built in the time of the Incas and they laughed at the question, repeating what I have said, that they were built before the Incas reigned. However, they had heard from their forbears that all that was there had appeared overnight. Because of this, and because they also say that bearded men were seen on the island of Titicaca (probably The Island of the Sun) it might have been there were people in these parts, come from where no one knows, before the Incas ruled. They may have perished in the wars.

Wendell C. Bennett, in his *Ancient Arts of the Andes* (the Museum of Modern Art, New York, 1954) says that the site of Tiahuanaco was certainly the most elaborate one and the purest manifestation of the culture yet to be found:

It is composed of a series of construction units spread out over an immense area. Although each unit is symmetrical within itself, no geometric system can be discovered in the over-all plan. The largest construction is a partially artificial stepped pyramid, called Acapana, once stone faced. The ground plan is 690 feet square and the height 50 feet. The flat top has house foundations and a large reservoir with a dressed-stone overflow. Acapana has every appearance of a fortified hill which could have served as a place of refuge in times of siege.

The addresses Peta had given me came in useful, not only to

get a room that was comfortable, but to gain entrance into the spare ranks of American and Peruvian and Bolivian archaeologists who were staying at Tiahuanaco village. I found myself after dinner that night in the company of archaeological students who had been only a week in the area and were, therefore, full of theories in a place which has caused people to voice the most startling theories for centuries. Everyone had what he, or she, thought was a novel observation to make. Guesses about the age and origin of the place were many and various. Many of the students declared that Tiahuanaco was the cradle not only of American civilization, but of the civilization of the world, and some established archaeologists, to whom they appealed for corroboration or contradiction, merely smiled enigmatically. The truth is that no one can prove his theory, whatever it is, though the most learned experts like Alden Mason, the great American anthropologist and archaeologist, with whom I had fascinating conversations later at Machu Picchu, can support their judgements with logic and solid evidence based on excavations and discovery of artifacts. Mason, in fact, told me that the Incas certainly had a separate existence for a long period in America itself but he was definitely of the opinion that man " did not originate in America itself because America never held any of his relatives, the anthropoid apes." Nor did it " reveal any remains of early and primitive human species." There are, of course, others who are adamant that civilizations which appeared in the Andean highlands and in the arid coastal plains of Peru as well as in the tropical jungles of Central America were at first unknown to, or even unsuspected by, east or west until the sixteenth century. The most frequent contrary theory voiced was that there had been early transoceanic migrations to and from America, some from Asia through the Bering Straits, in late glacial times. One who supported this theory said she had been to the site of the discovery of human footwear about 9,000 years old in a cave in Oregon. Several of the archaeological students retold the story of the amazing journey of a raft from Callao, Lima's port in Peru, to the Polynesian Tuamoto Islands and said such voyages supported the theories of those who postulated transoceanic migrations from Peru. There was a serious belief that the Polynesians were Incas, led by their ruler Tiki.

Some archaeologists did not believe that Columbus discovered America but suggested that when he persuaded Queen Isabella of Spain to finance his journey of discovery he withheld what he

knew, that the continent had already been discovered long before.
They believed that when he landed on 12th October, 1492 there
were already adventurers from Europe settled in South America.
They believed that the Norsemen had knowledge of the New
World some 550 years before the voyage of Christopher Columbus. There was, they said, documentary evidence in the form of
maps and diaries that the great explorer Lief Ericsson had discovered America in the eleventh century. But even the Vikings
might not have been first to set foot in the new world which they
had called Vinland because grapes grew there. Such theories of
early discovery found support among learned Peruvians who
believed that there had been unrecorded migrations from Europe.

Few believed that it had been possible, however, for these
migrants to make a return voyage to America because currents
and winds would be against them and would make navigation
difficult. The journey in both directions, to England from America
and from America to England, by an Englishman and an American in small boats in the summer of 1965 supported the theory of
die-hards that similar voyages in both directions between South
America and the Polynesian islands would have been possible by
unpowered craft.

The voyage of the Kon-tiki was cited to provide an explanation for some students why the sweet potato, of established
American origin, was discovered, by the very earliest European
explorers, growing under cultivation in Polynesia. The sweet
potato was stated to have long been known among the Polynesians.
They believed it to be an indigenous tuber. They called it
humara, which, though they did not know it, was its Peruvian
name. The potato was, of course, only one of the ' similarities '
between America and Polynesia.

There is, indeed, a strong legend among the Indians that Topa
Inca Yupanqui (1471-93) the tenth of the thirteen divine Inca
emperors, built a fleet of great rafts out of the trunks of trees
and that he fitted them with masts and sails and made a venture-
some voyage to some islands reputed to exist far off the Pacific
coast of Peru. The story goes that Topa Inca and his sailors discovered some islands, captured them and returned with some of
the black inhabitants as prisoners, and with gold and silver. Where
these islands were is a matter of conjecture, but the story gives
verisimilitude to the legend of the migrations. The Kon-tiki
raft which travelled from Peru to Tuamotu Islands in 1947 is said

to have been much like that used by Topa Inca, though I have looked in vain for positive proof that this was so. The early rafts were said to be trees bound together with forest bine such as is used to this day for the same purpose on the Amazon. Oars were used as well as sail. Some fifty men were carried on the rafts. My head was soon filled with the theories the students and archaeologists brought with them to the mysterious city and I felt in need of convalescence. At least of a refuge where I could sort out the conflicting ideas.

The archaeologist to whom Peta had given me a letter of introduction showed his affection for the young Peruvian by placing himself at my disposal. He was himself engaged in the writing of a book on the Incas about whom he had been doing research work for some two years.

"Can you believe it," he said, "that we know practically nothing about the mysterious people who lived here? We do not even know how many thousands of years ago. It is for that reason that the place is so fascinating, even glamorous. It is like a magnet to archaeological students, who are among the most theoretical people in the world today. It is a scandal, when so much money is being spent exploring Space that so little can be spared for excavating what could turn out to be the cradle of American civilization. Few really serious excavations have been made here, due mainly to the shortage of cash. When more excavations are carried out I believe great discoveries will be made, maybe, also, of gold and silver, human statuary, ceramics and pottery, so many things."

When I asked him why the original occupants of that site did not live near Titicaca, where there would have been cheap transport by Balsas he showed me three maps, drawn by indifferent cartographers over the ages, all of which showed the lake coming right up to the site.

"Titicaca," he said, "has receded over the centuries. The superstitious Indians will tell you that the lake is bottomless and that the water seeps away into the Pacific. It is very deep, but hardly as deep as that."

When I asked my friend how he accounted for the destruction of so substantial a place, built as it had been of stone blocks weighing a hundred tons, he said that an earthquake could have been responsible but that it was also possible that the place was overrun by invaders. The Incas, who had their legendary origin on the Island of the Sun on Titicaca, had ruled Chile as well as

B*

Peru, and had for certain conquered Bolivia, probably by 1315, and ruled the country for 200 years, until 1538.

What interested me most in the many statements he made to me was that some experts linked up Tiahuanaco with Cuzco and believed that the Incas developed in the former place and then migrated as the just Inca, Manco Capac, was supposed to have done. A well-known writer named Blas Valera, whose writings have been lost for many years but whose statements had been quoted earlier by reliable writers said that the Incas had reigned over Tiahuanaco many hundreds of years before Manco Capac was supposed to have moved from Titicaca to Cuzco. He regarded Sinchi Roca, the son of Manco Capac, a legendary or a historical figure (and some support the one, some the other theory), as the first Inca. Sinchi Roca was certainly the first to bear the royal title of Sapa Inca. The author Montesinos, quoting Blas Valera, declared that there had probably been not thirteen, but over a hundred Incas before the capital of Cuzco was founded. The inference was that Tiahuanaco was the original home of the Incas, a convenient and a comforting theory. If it could be proved, which it cannot be, it would solve the great mystery which is exercising so many great minds. The people who support the theory say that the Incas consolidated their power after migrating to the Cuzco Valley where they soon began to extend a terrific influence over a vast area. The Incas conquered other rival tribes, regarding the campaigns at first mainly as a religious crusade. It is said that they were eventually accepted as the rulers of the Andes, and of the coast. They were regarded by all as god-emperors.

The archaeologist tried to set Tiahuanaco against the background of the world as it was thought to be in Asia and Europe before the birth of Christ.

According to a map of the world drawn by Hecatæus (500 B.C.) the territory then known to man took the shape of an embryo baby in its mother's womb. The map showed the Mediterranean Sea with, pressed around it, a narrow area marked Europa to the north; and Libya to the south as far as the southern outlet to the Red Sea; and Iberes to the west; and a compact piece of Asia from the Red Sea, including the Euphrates, Tigris and Indus, to the Caucasus, in the east. Eratosthenes (220 B.C.) drew a map of the world that was very much like that of his predecessor but with the addition of India and Scythia, and, to the north of Europe,

Brettania and Baltia. I could not for the life of me imagine what either of these primitive cartographers would have said had they been told that 2,000 years before they drew these still-surviving maps, when civilizations in Asia, Egypt and Greece had been the entire world—so they thought—great aboriginal cultures had similarly been developing on a then unknown continent on the other side of the world. Naturally, the peoples in America also thought there were no other cultures but their own. What it means is that 5,000 years ago, on opposite sides of the world, two entirely independent cultures had developed, at times on amazingly parallel lines. There are many theories about migrations over the ice cap from Asia to America, and of voyages to America before those carried out by the Norsemen or by Christopher Columbus but there is no evidence of any real cultural contacts such as would justify the parallel development.

In the Andes and on the coast of Peru cultures known as Tiahuanaco, Chavin and Paracas, to mention three, produced great buildings and products of ceramics and textiles. They were great craftsmen in gold and silver, which precious metals were found in vast quantities. They knew something about astronomy. They were able to measure time. They even developed agriculture, sometimes to the most advanced stage by using remarkably clever systems of irrigation canals. They left behind many examples of fine masonry, carving, polychrome ornaments, textiles (tapestry), bronze ornaments, weapons and tools.

That night I lay awake mulling over some of the sensational theories I had heard expressed. As an amateur who had read a considerable amount about the early civilizations on my way through South America, beginning with my fortuitous encounter with Peta and her husband, I wanted to be able to link up Tiahuanaco with Cuzco. It would be so easy to conceive one dominant culture, no matter how many off-shoots there had been, flowing from the dim mists of time right down to the arrival of history between 1524 and 1528. The trouble is that what is plausible and even likely is not always correct.

One thing was certain, I told myself, and that is that millions of other people had been entirely inaccurate in believing that there was absolutely no parallel in the world to the earliest Mediterranean civilizations. It was clear that as long as 5,000 years ago, when civilizations in Asia, Egypt and Greece thought of themselves as comprising the entire world, great aboriginal cultures had risen quite independently in South America which also assumed that they comprised the whole universe. In both these widely separated areas, completely unknown to each other, quite separate civilizations continued to flourish at least up to 2,000 years ago. Probably 1,000 years before Babylon began to flower, when it was but a wilting seedling in the sand, the first of a succession of remarkable civilizations was starting to develop in the high Andes, spreading on to the desert coast, then to the jungles of Central and South America. Both these civilizations, so widely separated, excelled in architecture, in the manfacture of textiles (tapestry) and pottery. In both these widely separated civilizations cameloid animals were used for transport.

Such intimate matters as religion showed almost identical devices by which to capture converts, though the religion of the northern hemisphere had become Christian and that of the southern hemisphere remained heathen. The early American civilizations accepted totemism. They worshipped animals, like the condor, the puma and the snake and they also worshipped plants and stones. The ancient Peruvians believed they were descended from the condor or the jaguar or even from rivers and lakes. These protective spirits were given the generic name *Huaca*, which meant " mysterious holy powers ". Where the Incas took over they developed the cult of the sun, the Peruvian name for which was *Inti* or *Apu-Punchau* (the head of day). They thought the sun had human form, as people today believe their god has human form. The Incas came to believe that they were descended from *Inti*. The Incas did not suppress all the cults older than that of the sun and the moon, whether held by ancient forbears at Tiahuanaco or by other tribes. They retained especially two great gods whom they put in their pantheon—*Viracocha* (" the foam of the lake "), which was most certainly the figure of the weeping god seen on the Gate of the Sun, and *Pachacamac* (" he who animates the earth "). The Incas believed that Inti, after crossing the sky, warming the icy winds of the Andes and the Altiplano, plunged into the western sea, which he nearly dried up. He swam back to earth and when he reappeared next sunrise he was rejuvenated by his bath. Viracocha, the central figure on the Gateway of the Sun, was identified with rain and thunder, fertility and creation. The cult of the dead, as in early Egypt, occupied a high place in religion. A great sanctity attached to the mortal remains of human forbears. The burial rites of ancient Egypt and ancient Peru were

in several particulars similar. The Egyptian process of mummifi-
cation was similar to the process in Peru, although the mummified
body was arranged differently. It lay horizontally in Egypt but it
was given a sitting posture in Peru. In both places mummies were
wrapped in textiles. The mummies of the Incas were kept in the
Great Sun Temple at Cuzco which is where they were seen by the
Spanish vandals. They were carried annually in ceremonial
parades at festivals of honour of the dead.

So parallel was the development in totally different fields that
one anthropologist formed the theory that ancient Egypt may
have had an influence on pre Inca cultures. The desert kingdom
of the Mochicas, with that of the Chimus, whom the Incas
defeated fifty years before the Spanish invaders came, were said
culturally to belong approximately to the same age as Pompeii.
When artifacts from the two cultures, 6,000 miles apart and
entirely unconnected, were minutely examined they were found to
be as identical as twin children. It seemed as if the two civilizations, instead of being entirely unknown to each other, had been
in close liaison. Had, in fact, used the same craftsmen.

Maybe, I thought, as I lay restlessly in bed, some anthropologist would one day draw startling conclusions from the fact that
two entirely different types of *homo sapiens*, separated by a vast
ocean thought to be unnavigable by such craft as then existed,
could develop along such similar lines despite that they were supposed to be ethnically dissimilar.

I had been brought up to think that the ancient world was
centred on the Near East. Now, if anyone talked to me about
Babylon, Egypt or Greece I would retaliate with such names as
Nazca, Chavin, Mochica, Paracas and Tiahuanaco, all connected
with Peru, as well as other American cultures, the Mayas, the
Toltecs, the Aztecs. It seemed to me now that the Incas, however
old their civilization may be, organized, wittingly or unwittingly,
a mass renaissance of the many earlier civilizations on the backs of
which they reached great heights. The pre Inca civilizations may
have been united by the Incas in one great mysterious empire. It
was unfortunate that we knew few of the names of the cultures
which shaped the pre Inca civilizations, especially as scholars, like
Alden Mason, have always maintained that real history is a record
of the lives of a few great men and that history does not exist
apart from biography.

V

Island of the Sun

GUAQUI, A small port twelve miles beyond Tiahuanaco's ruined city, was crowded when I arrived there at the start of my journey to Cuzco. There were thousands of pure Indians and their bowler hatted, brilliantly shawled and voluminously petticoated women, and each couple seemed to tend tightly herded flocks of hauty llamas and vicunas. At the corners of the narrow streets old wizened squaws squatted on their haunches on rough straw matting selling coca leaves which everyone chewed as regularly as they breathed. There were a few small ships inshore and dozens of sailing vessels and small balsas, or single manned fishing boats, made from reeds. As, thirsty for more legends of the Incas, I tried to find Peta's favourite boatman, I met the inevitable Bolivian who had emigrated to America and been deported. His breath smelled strongly for he had obviously imbibed heavily of a favourite Chincha intoxicant made from quinoa.

" You not Americano," he said in tones of accusation as if I was impersonating the prince of the world.

" No, English," I replied stoutly.

" English," he repeated, uncertain what next to say. " You really English. Eh! "

The man turned and called out something in Quechua and several of his men paused and stared at me. Then the emigrant spoke again and everyone laughed. Laughter is a rare sound in Bolivia. On the very few occasions I heard it, I wheeled round in surprise, but always to find someone embarrassed or in pain. I do not think I ever saw many smile pleasantly with their lips let alone with their eyes. Eyes here are deep set, remote, cold. Other Indians, passing with their loaded llamas—the only beast of burden on the Altiplano—halted their animals and looked at me with unaffected interest.

" What have you told them?" I asked irritably.

" It is joke," said the Indian trying to pacify me in the hope that he would be rewarded. " Do you not know joke of your queen?"

It was then, for the first time, but by no means the last, I heard the time-honoured Bolivian joke, not about Queen Elizabeth II, but about Queen Victoria. It was really a satirical jibe at the one-time readiness of the British to practise gun-boat diplomacy.

Queen Victoria was apparently once given cause for anger when, during a Bolivian revolution, or as a result of one, the Bolivians caused her plenipotentiary to be chased out of La Paz in a state of pure nature seated on a donkey. Victoria, no more educated in geography than her subjects, despite the possession of a vast Empire, ordered the standard treatment. A gun-boat was sent forthwith to shell Bolivia. The captain made speedily for the Pacific coast of South America only to find to his astonishment that Bolivia had no coast. He signalled back to the Queen that his shells would not reach the capital of the landlocked nation. Victoria, full of pique, had Bolivia immediately erased from the map that hung in her study.

When the emigrant and his cronies had had their fill of the joke at Britain's expense, I asked him about the facilities for crossing the lake. The lake possessed five vessels, the largest 760 tons and the smallest 150 tons, maintained by the Peruvian Transport Corporation.

The emigrant took me to one side and pointed out an old steamboat bearing in faded letters, the name *Yavari,* which was preparing to leave.

" That was made in Britain," he said aloud.

I thought the man was continuing to joke and ignored the remark, but he repeated it in earnest tones.

" But Bolivia is landlocked," I replied. " How could any ship from Britain reach this inland sea? Does it have wheels? Did it come overland?"

The vessel was a tanker of about 200 tons and the very idea of it steaming up the Altiplano from the coast, over one of the roughest and steepest mountainous terrains in the continent, brought smiles and ribaldry from all. How could it possibly reach the highest navigable water in the world at a height of 13,290 feet?

" But you want to bet? You English are sports, yes? You bet

me it was not built in Britain? That it was sent here by your countrymen? That it did not come over the mountains?"

This joke was somehow linked with Queen Victoria and her ignorance of the topography of Bolivia, so I said nothing. But it was no joke. The *Yarvari* was built in the Scottish shipyard by Cammel Laird in 1862, and was the first steamer to cross the lake. The vessel was sent under its own steam to the nearest port on the Pacific coast. It was then taken to pieces and carried up into, and over, the Andes to Titicaca. Some of it was transported on the backs of llamas. The pieces were then put together again from a Meccano-like plan and the ship was launched. A few years later a second ship came. Even after being given full details of this amazing amphibious operation, and assured on oath of the Incas that every syllable was true I did not believe it. The seamen of landlocked Bolivia, squat, burnished-faced men with clumsy, barrel-chested figures that accommodated the most overdeveloped lungs in the world, stared at me annoyed. The feat they assured me was performed under the direction of an American named Henry Meiggs, the first do-it-yourself railway engineer, who, without orthodox training, planned and built the Central Railway. Meiggs apparently got into serious financial trouble during the Californian Gold Rush and fled to South America where he proceeded to astonish orthodox engineers with his skills.

Meiggs had many faults, not the least a trickster's brain, but he also possessed imagination and drive and the secret of man-management. Whatever he had done wrong in the United States he compensated for in the pioneer days of Peru and Bolivia.

I found Peta's old boatman and he was delighted to get news of his favourite client. His son was moving all his belongings from the hovel in which he had lived alone since the death of his wife to a spare room in a new bungalow but he agreed " for Peta's sake " to take me to the Island of the Sun. As we drank coffee on the shore of the lake he showed me a sheaf of letters of thanks he had received from people, some of whom he claimed were professors and heads of governments. They all regarded the Island of the Sun, he said, as a sacred place, the scene of the origin of the world. He had been born beside the lake and knew all its traditions. In fact he was obsessed with the Island of the Sun and the thousand and one strange legends connected with the origin there of the Inca dynasty. I suspected at times that after he had collected all the folklore he had begun to make up other stories to maintain his position as "the greatest authority on the Island of the Sun."

Trying to wean him off the legends, I mentioned Titicaca which interested me far more.

"It's supposed to be bottomless," I observed.

"That hasn't prevented people from trying to drag it to find gold," he said.

The most persistent story about the lake, he told me, was that the Incas went back to the place of their dynastic birth, on the Island of the Sun, when the Spanish brigands arrived, and threw into the water vast stores of gold from the temple and from the Palace of the Nustas on the Island of the Coati. They would have done anything rather than allow the treasure to fall into the hands of the hated invaders. Many efforts had been made since, the last fairly recently, to recover the gold, but the lake was too deep even if it was not connected with the Pacific as the Indians declared. The bed had been touched at one point only, 1,500 feet down. The lake was fed by twenty-five rivers, among them the Tiahuanaco, named after the ancient city. It was clear from the attitude of the Indians to the lake that this vast sheet of water was a *huaca,* or sacred place, the centre of eternal mystery.

As we left the shore for the island in his ornate boat in the sunlight of a golden day, the old man pointed out various ships on which he had served or travelled. Titicaca's fleet consisted of, besides the *Yavari* and the *Upura,* both about a century old, three twin-screw passenger vessels, the *Ollanta,* the *Inca* and the *Coya.* The *Ollanta,* the most popular craft, crossed the vast lake twice each week at night in both directions between Guaqui and Puno, the Peruvian port on the north-west shore. From Puno I could go on one of the most remarkable railways of South America to Cuzco, the ancient imperial capital of the Incas. He seemed to know the captains and the mates of all the craft and took care to salute them, but he knew also by their nicknames all the members of the crew.

"They're a brave lot of men," he said, "and as strong as any race anywhere in the world. Some of them are first-class fighters and if they could survive down there "—he pointed his thumb downwards—" they would beat the living daylight out of your world champion boxers and wrestlers. Trouble is they wouldn't be any use at sea level any more than people used to sea level would be any use up here on top of the world."

As we moved quietly across Titicaca, seeing shoals of fish turn swiftly from the boat, and watching great flocks of sea fowl wheel and dive to the accompaniment of evil cackles, I felt that I was going to the source of the great mystery—the unexplained appearance at a time which was as backward as the Stone Age of a race of men who seemed to be born already endowed with great skills and accomplishments. Certainly this island must have been visited by thousands of men in search of some explanation and to have been the scene of their disappointment. There is no contemporary source of early Peruvian history. There are no written records of the Incas for the reason that they could not write. What has come down to us, apart from the writings of Spanish conquerors and their like, has been derived from inanimate objects, buried cities, pottery, silver and gold and implements, the most eloquent of these being the *quipa*, which the Incas used for accountancy. All that we had in plenty were the legends such as the boatman told.

The Island of the Sun, much venerated by all the Indians for reasons they do not always understand, is regarded as the birthplace of the first Inca, Manco Capac. When I asked the old man to tell me about Manco Capac he produced a much-thumbed copy of a painting of the god-emperor by the Croatian-Peruvian artist, Kristian Krekovich, and handed it to me as if that would explain everything. The portrait is the most impressive representation of man I have ever seen. Manco Capac is depicted as a man of steel with a great condor on his much bangled forearm, a supernatural creature, combining in his fearsome features the strength and will of both man and god, a creature who obviously draws his power from all the known forces of the universe and all the occult forces of hell. He was at once the invincible warrior, the all-knowing judge, the demon king. He had no equal anywhere.

On the back of the portrait in Spanish were the words, " The rapid expansion [of the Inca Empire] constituted one of the most astounding facts of history. It began in 1438 under Pachacuti [the ninth Inca] and reached its height in 1493 under Tupac Yupanqui. In half a century father and son extended their dominions from northern Ecuador to the central zone of Chile. The feats of these two Incas may be compared, with no argument whatsoever, with those of the greatest warriors and kings of other parts of the world . . ." The Spanish writer, Garcilaso, says that Capac and his sister, Mama Ocllo, were created by the Sun, which is the personification of the almighty god of creation, and deposited on the Island of the Sun, a place which today, as I discovered, has no clue to the divinity of its original occupant. Another version says that Capac emerged from the depths of Titicaca with Ocllo. The almighty god of creation had no great opinion of men already living on earth and he sent Capac and Ocllo to teach them the arts of civilization, a task, judging from the present day occupants of the earth, he did not accomplish. Many archaeologists had tried, as I did, and failed to find any clue that would prove a link between the Island of the Sun and the Incas. There is no evidence on the island, or indeed, round the shores of Titicaca, that the Inca civilization began there.

The story told to me by a 90-year-old self-taught archaeologist on the Island of the Sun is that the first Inca, Manco Capac, and his sister, Mama Ocllo, left the island and travelled through the mountains to Cuzco, actually along the route I had already planned to take. His father had instructed him to stab the earth at brief intervals along the way with the gold staff he had to carry and not to pause until the staff sank into the earth. The journey lasted for some years. On the way Capac and Ocllo co-habited as a result of which a child, to be known as Sinchi Roca, and to become the second Inca, was born. The staff sank into the fertile earth in a valley which was the centre of the world, Qosqo or Cuzco, and here Manco built his house on the site of the later Temple of the Sun, Tawantinsuyo. The Inca Empire was founded, its huge territory covering a total area of two million square miles. The local tribes were driven out. According to another legend Manco's four sisters accompanied him. The Incas could marry no woman but their sisters. The children born to them are said to have displayed the attributes of superiority ascribed, until enlightened times, to the most cretinous offspring of royalty.

I can imagine no more pleasant way of spending a sunny afternoon than to visit the Island of the Sun, especially in the company of so good a raconteur as the old Indian, but it is necessary to take care lest one returns with a wholly romanticized idea of its place in the life of the Incas.

VI

The Water People

OF ALL the 7,000,000 Indians in the Andean region the most remarkable are the Urus, or Uru-Chipaya, whom I saw on Titicaca next day. They are probably the only people in the world who derive all the necessities of life from one plant, the tortora reed, which grows round the edges of the inland sea.

As I travelled on the Altiplano, and, later, near the Amazon, I came to realize how backward were the Quechua and Aymara Indians in spite of all the efforts made to drag them into the twentieth century. When I saw the Urus, however, I knew that the others were, by comparison, living in modern times. In some remote parts I saw primitive agriculturalists using the digging stick and hoe in ways which would have been considered out of date in the time of Christ. Farmers who used the more advanced ox-drawn ploughs considered themselves highly advanced. Although fire-arms were a necessity for one's defence in Bolivia, where lawlessness breaks out without warning, I did not see many modern fire-arms in use in the remoter parts of Bolivia or Peru, though they were undoubtedly used for poaching. Slings and bolas, which had been used by the Incas for catching alpacas and llamas, still the favourite animals, were said to be used to this day for catching vicunas.

Villages I visited were comprised of adobe houses and the inhabitants earned their living making pottery, weaving, and, in the summer, by agriculture. The old men weaved with the treadles and the women with the girdle-backed tension loom. Most of the clothes made and worn reminded one of the days of the Incas. The Indians wore thick clothes with knitted caps and ear muffs for protection against the night cold and the peasant women dressed gaily in voluminous petticoats. Both men and women wore ponchos, some of them in gay colours. Usually each large village had a communal building made of adobe in which the inhabitants gathered to celebrate anniversaries. Music was provided by such instruments as the drum, gongs, panpipes and flutes. Always a headman presided, sometimes accompanied by a medicine man.

The Urus have apparently decided that they cannot keep pace with civilization and for that reason they have retreated far on to Lake Titicaca. They want to avoid meeting modern man. Their original home was on that part of the Altiplano between Titicaca and the Pacific and it is not known exactly when they moved from it as a community to live on the water. When they lived on land they felt isolated, even from the Aymara and the Quechua Indians. The tribe has never been able to communicate fully with anyone. Their language puzzles even philologists who never cease to argue about its origin. It bears little resemblance to Aymara or Quechua. People who have tried to master it by living with the Urus have said that it was easy to learn but had a limited range. The Urus baffled them even more than the language. There were no words for objects which had come into being in the past several hundred years.

The Urus are dirty. They are said to dislike water, though I saw some of them swimming. Their children look emaciated and do not go to school. In spite of their poverty the Urus are fiercely independent. To live on Titicaca this considerable community had to use their ingenuity. They had to make their own islands—floating islands, made of thick mats woven out of tortora reeds and placed one on top of another to a great depth until the top one floated above the surface of the water. The top mat may remain dry only for a couple of weeks but when it became saturated and began to submerge the women put down a new mat. So they went on month after month throughout the year. The water is deep and the depth of the islands is considerable: their amazing buoyancy is such that the islands can carry not only the house for a large family (this is also made out of tortura reeds), but also outhouses for storage or in which to keep pets, hens, vizcacha, dogs and even little black pigs. The Urus obtain these pets in barter transactions for their surplus fish. Even the boats in which the Urus go fishing or hunting—they kill wild fowl with sling shots—are made not of wood but of tortora reeds. The boats, like the mats for the islands, last only a few weeks until they are saturated and then have to be replaced. There are plenty of bulrushes to weave into another boat. The balsas are of varying size. The largest, used by as many as thirty people to commute between the islands of friends or relatives, are fitted with efficient sails, also woven out of tortura reeds. Today there are some wooden boats fitted with outboard motors. The water Indians grow vegetables on the islands by placing seeds deep into the matting where they germinate and take root. Some of the tastiest potatoes are said to be grown on these floating islands. One of the vegetables most enjoyed with the potatoes are the tender green shoots of the tortora reeds.

People who deplore the way of life of the Urus do not realize that they are blissfully happy. They have plenty of free sport, fishing and hunting. They do not have to pay taxes. They carry out no enforced work like some other Indians. They are completely free and enjoy good health in spite of the severity of the winter. If they are ill they do not have a Health Service, but they do have their own medicine men. These amateurs use herbs which grow around Titicaca. The chief medicine men, who call themselves *curanderos,* are credited with a wide knowledge of medicine based on traditional remedies handed down through the family. Some of the more unscrupulous *curanderos* prescribe magical potions for all purposes, from barrenness in women to blindness and insanity. Each housewife has her own remedy for everyday ailments. Some of the older women cling to witches' brews made from the intestines of nocturnal animals, or from tails, paws, skins, shells and even blood.

VII

Cameloids in Peru

IT WAS not until I reached Puno, a busy port of some 25,000 people on the north-west shore of Titicaca, that I realized the important part the llamas, and other cameloid animals, play in the economy of the Altiplano. It was market day and the population seemed to have doubled with the influx of Indians and their squaws from a thickly populated outlying area. The llamas were busy carrying loads of yarn to the waiting transports for Lima, where it would be made up into knitted articles. It was fascinating to see with what nonchalance the strange animals threaded their way through the noisy crowds.

An American who had obviously more than an amateur interest in zoology halted beside a particularly fine pack of llamas and pointed out to me some of their finer points. He had recently been in Egypt, he said, and it puzzled him that the cameloid llama and its distant relative, the camel, should have played such a vital part (and such similar roles) in the economies of two widely separated, but in many ways similar, countries. As he pointed out to me with the skill of a show judge the various physical flaws in the necks of the animals he told me in asides that the llama was native to Peru. Remains of llamas were found on the Peruvian coastal plain over a millenium ago. The animals had been employed as a means of transport as early as 5000 B.C. and just as they were used today. They had then, as now, carried burdens of up to a hundred pounds and at the pace of ten miles a day. Like the camel, the llama had been used in the making of sacrifices to propitiate the gods. They had also been used both in Peru and Egypt by seers to foretell the future.

Both animals had the same practical uses in their respective countries. Cameloid dung for instance provided an efficient fuel

where wood and coal were scarce. The camel had been represented at the strength of a cavalry corps in the army of Xerxes
when Greece was invaded in 482 B.C. despite that the animal did
not seem to have made its appearance in the area of the Nile,
thought to be its home, until 400 B.C. Both camel and llama had
the advantage in desert or in barren areas, of being able to travel
for long distances where water and food were scarce. The zoolo-
gist thought the Peruvians had developed the llamas from guana-
cos, an animal which grew to seven feet tall.

But for the American I would not have met in any number
Peru's most charming cameloid, the vicuna, an orange-red little
animal which is very rare and in danger of becoming extinct. It
is also related to the guanaco from which it differs by inferior
stature, by a more elegant and slender build, and by the absence
of bare callosities on the hind limbs. The vicuna are mercilessly
hunted by poachers in the high Andes where they live at incredible altitudes. Just outside Puno a farmer had set up a large
vicuna ranch, the only one of its kind in Peru, with the encourage-
ment of the government. I was taken along to see it. The American told me, with the eagerness of a guide, that the wool of the
vicuna was much coveted. It was soft and warm and also had
what he called a quality appearance. He said that the Incas, in
the heyday of the empire, made it unlawful for anyone but nobles
to wear tunics made from the wool. Vicuna wool was much in
demand now by fashion houses in America. Fabulous prices were
paid for it. A gentleman in films in America was said to have a
vicuna overcoat which had cost £120. Even rich merchants in
Peruvian towns boasted native ponchos made of vicuna wool which
had cost £50.

The ranch was carefully guarded, especially at night, against
poachers, and I understood why when the farmer told us that he
had 450 precious animals, young and old. The vicunas were a
peculiar combination of fragility and strength, robust health and
high susceptibility to parasitic disease. They were at home in the
lowest temperatures, 16,000 feet up in the Andes where they were
born. Even infant animals survived some of the worst storms ever
known, yet they seemed to enjoy the heat of the sun. The farmer
had begun the venture to try to breed vicunas in captivity. He also
wanted to domesticate them, as the llama and the guanaco had
been domesticated. He had in mind the possibility of increasing
the yield of wool, of which the vicuna produced slightly less than

a pound a year. Already success had rewarded his efforts. He had bred from several pairs and the infants, which looked like children's toys, were doing well.

"Such ranches as this could save the vicuna from extinction," the American told me, and he knew what he was talking about. He had a set of figures showing how the animals had declined in numbers in post-war years. He finally confessed that he had come to Peru primarily to study the cameloid animals. He was going to an important seminary that had been organized at Arequipa at the foot of El Misti. Delegates from Peru, the Argentine and Bolivia were meeting to discuss legislation passed by their respective governments to preserve the animals. Much of the legislation conflicted and resulted in an effect opposite to that which was aimed at. The governments all wished to control the sale of vicuna wool but one of them, Bolivia, though it protected the vicuna in its own country, allowed the manufacture and export of luxury goods " made from imported vicuna wool ". The amount of goods exported a year represented vicuna wool weighing between four and six tons. This meant, said the American, that at least 50,000 vicunas were killed somewhere every year. Peru suspected that most of this wool was obtained by poaching in the high mountains, on, or near to, the Peruvian-Bolivian frontier, where the animals were to be found in large numbers. Poachers could there operate from isolated villages with a reasonable degree of success and link up with other poachers on the other side of the frontier. He suspected that the poachers had organized a " trade route " to La Paz which was unfrequented by ordinary travellers. Vicuna wool was then made up into a range of luxury goods for sale in America.

One of the attendants on the farm told me that he had spent six years in the Andes at this point trying to learn the secrets of the poachers.

"They climb like goats," he said. " They move silently as ghosts. They don't use the gun. That would give them away. The cast the bolas—a weight tied to a rope—and bring the animals down by lassooing their legs. That is a trick that has come down to them from poachers in Inca days. There have been as many as three of us on patrol in an area favourable for poaching. We have never allowed our vigil to lapse for a moment. Yet we had reason to believe the next morning that a gang of poachers had been at work under our very noses and had secured a fine bag."

The animals are extraordinarily lithe and speedy. Some of them are able even to elude the bolas. In more remote parts, where the poachers rely on their isolation, the animals are shot with sporting rifles fitted with telescopic sights.

The American estimated that there were fewer than 600,000 vicunas alive today, and all of them in the Andes. They had existed in millions until the Spanish marauders came into the country. The Incas had protected the animals but the Spaniards, with their notorious attitude to dumb animals, had promiscuously slaughtered them. But for the fact that the vicunas were elusive and could climb on to the highest crags they would have been extinct like the dodo, long ago. The only hope for their continued existence, as one of the beautiful animals in the world, lay in the possibility that other nature lovers would organize vicuna ranches. Already the annual death rate of the animal from parasitic diseases was alarmingly high.

The American had something good to say of all the cameloids when we met again over a drink on the terrace of our hotel. The llama was the most untiring beast of burden. Llama skins, measuring 6 feet by 5 feet for use as rugs or bed covers were priced at £36. The alpaca produced some 4,000 tons of wool a year. The vicuna, apart from the value of its wool, was one of the most lovable animals in the world. Incidentally, an Austrian emigree he knew had crossed a vicuna with an alpaca to produce a hybrid called pacovicuna. The alpaca had also been crossed with a llama to produce a huarizo. In each case the production of wool had been increased but the hybrids inherited the vices of both animals.

There was a time when the only animals of burden in Peru were cameloids. It was for this reason that the Inca roads were narrow. There were no horse-drawn carts. When the Spaniards arrived with their horses the Incas were astonished to see animals so large and strong. Now, in addition to the 2,758,730 llamas, alpacas and vicunas, there are in Peru over a million horses and mules. There are also nearly four million cattle in addition to 14,016,000 sheep, 4,300,000 goats and 1,370,000 pigs.

VIII

By Rail to Cuzco

EVEN MORE astonishing than English ships, which came over the Andes from the sea after travelling from Britain to ply for over a century on the highest navigable lake in the world, was an " English railway " instituted as long ago as 1890. It is still operating also in the Andes.

Truth to tell I did not expect to find a train of any kind at Puno (altitude 12,648 feet), least of all one which would carry me through the mountains (and several bouts of sirochi, or height sickness) to Cuzco, imperial capital of the Incas, 11,440 feet above sea level. I suppose I had not done my homework: I had anticipated a dreadful journey by road along the same track that Manco Capac had taken.

I learned of the " English railway " when I visited a travel office in Puno and met a superannuated railway official. He had started his long life on the railway which ran from Callao, the port, to Lima, the capital, a distance of only nine miles. He proudly claimed that this short line, later extended to Chorillos, was the first standard gauge railway in all South America, though, as I learned later, it preceded the completion of lines in Brazil and Chile only by a few months. It was inaugurated in 1851 at a time when railways were things only to dream about in Asia, Oceania and Africa. He had started to work on the Callao-Lima line as a boy with an oil can and had remained on it until it was replaced by the Lima tramway system. Then he had come to work as an overseer on the Southern railway, which, together with the Central railway, he called the " English railway " because the English took it over, lock, stock and barrel in 1890. Apparently both lines were begun by President Balta (1868-72), who had a small boy's enthusiasm for trains, an enthusiasm which, in his term of office cost £37,500,000. This was far more than Peru was worth. To get out of debt the Peruvian government signed an agreement with a British corporation, under which it assumed responsibilities for the Peruvian debt in return for the right to operate Peru's railways for a period of sixty-six years. The agreement was modified in recent times but the British company continued to run the chief railways in Peru. My informant was a great admirer of Britain, mainly because of its achievements in railway engineering.

Britain was the pioneer in the building of domestic railway networks and was consequently consulted by countries all over the world who wished to have railway systems of their own. Just over a decade earlier Britain had expanded rapidly and built many of its major trunk lines. Officials of South American governments came to London eager to avail themselves of British industrial facilities, British know-how in railway engineering and British capital. The British government authorized £129,000,000 for railway expansion by British companies in 1846 alone. While Britain was helping South America to build railways the United States was still developing its own system. The first transcontinental link in the U.S.A. was not completed until 1869. British investment in South America rose steadily. Nearly half of it was in railways.

" Peru's interest in railways," the ex-overseer told me, " dates from the visit Simon Bolivar paid to England in 1810. He took a ride on a short railway operating at a colliery in the North and became an enthusiast for the Iron Horse."

Simor Bolivar's government sought tenders for the building of the Lima-Callao line as early as 1826. There were difficulties. The second bid was made in 1834. It was not until 1850 that the work was begun, and by the same President who put an end to slavery in Peru. Most of the rolling stock and the equipment, including the signals system, were made in Britain, and some of it is preserved as examples of fine workmanship. Two of the chief engineers were British. The first two railway engines were given names, as are engines in Britain. Many of the regulations in vogue in Britain were adopted.

I was delighted to find that I could get a ticket to travel from Puno on Titicaca to Cuzco after changing at Juliaco, which is the highland centre for collecting and tanning animal hides. The Southern railway climbs into the mountains from the Pacific by a gradual, easy grade which requires no switchbacks and has only one tunnel. This is quite a contrast to the Central railway, which is the highest standard gauge in the world. The railway climbs from sea level at Callao to 15,693 feet in just over a hundred miles. On its way the railway passes through sixty-five tunnels and fifteen zigzags where the trains have to be reversed in order to be able to continue the ascent. To reach Juliaco, from the coast, the train has to wind its way round two volcanoes, Misti and Chachani. The scene changes from bare mountains to fertile pampa.

The journey to Cuzco is full of interest and enabled me to get an insight into the simple economy of the highlands where Indian women still carry on the tradition of slavery in Peru. They perform at least three jobs at the same time, and not for eight, but eighteen hours a day. They tend flocks of llamas and alpacas and sheep even as they look after their numerous children. When a train arrives they become the most pathetic saleswomen in the world. They try to persuade passengers to buy pottery, furs, foot-muffs and slippers made of alpaca skin as well as rugs, ponchos, ceramics, cakes and " Inca souvenirs ". The pottery, which has obviously just been fired in some primitive oven, is always " ancient ", dug up on the site of some " lost city ". The fur, which is fox, is always vicuna. The rugs are hand-made and represent years of hard work. It is obvious that the women are abysmally poor and cowed, but in spite of this they look sturdy and proud. They seemed to make as much money out of the people who photograph them as out of those who buy their wares. The women all wore the English bowler, grey or brown, or, in the case of young girls, red or yellow, and tipped them over their squinting, black eyes, like young bloods at the races in England. If they wore a poncho it was highly coloured. Sometimes there were traces of embroidery on their bodices and jewellery of antique appearance in their ears or on their fingers. Now and then we saw a few men herding the llamas, but they always looked on from a distance. They were squat and barrel-chested. The ponchos they wore were belted so that they seemed to be wearing Inca tunics over knee-deep pantaloons. Some wore skimmer coolie hats but most of them wore coloured ear caps as a protection against the cold.

To go from Puno to Cuzco in dull weather is to pass from the hell of drab sterility to the heaven of abundant fertility, yet these two widely separated places have much in common. Peru is rich in folklore in which legends from the time of the Incas and customs from the Spanish marauders are nicely blended. In Puno and Cuzco, where the folklore is most abundant the inhabitants execute similar dances, wear similar apparel and display similarly individualistic styles. Both communities dress lavishly during Catholic festivals, which are partly pagan and partly superstitious. One dance which the two towns favour is the *huayno*. No one could tell me its origin or the story that it enshrines.

On my way to Cuzco, high up in the soaring Andes, I had the feeling at times that we were getting lost. To reach this ancient centre of a pagan empire we had to travel from Puno on Titicaca, one of the remoter places on earth, along a winding, tortuous track through the mighty mountains, into, and over, the clouds two miles high above the Pacific. The journey was arduous, but the scenes, all along the route, were exciting. At times I saw large flocks of llama, alpaca or vicuna watched over by bowler-hatted Indian squaws in highly coloured skirts and shawls many miles from any kind of habitation. The women nearly all had a baby tied in black cloth to their backs. If they did not have a baby they carried a heavy stone where the child would have been to give them the same balance. Some of the older women played pipes of Pan, an old Peruvian instrument, filling the icy air with plaintive Indian music. Sometimes in voices of amazing virtuosity that recalled to mind Yma Sumac, they cried out messages to relatives across the narrow valley or sang folk songs such as had been heard in the mountains for centuries. Some of the poorer women twisted into yarn wool straight from the backs of their animals.

The scenery was beautiful. One moment there was sublime majesty expressed in grandiose snowclad peaks and crests that were sharply outlined against the deep blue sky. Sometimes there was a whole chain of peaks that seemed to float in the air far above a deep belt of white mist. Sometimes there were verdant valleys in which flowering trees grew and Indian children played. Most stirring of all sights were the nightmarish shapes of the condor which I saw in the late afternoon hovering on blue and white wing spans up to 9 feet across as they searched the bleak pampas below for luscious meals of llama foal. There were also dread circuses of red-billed king vultures that described black circles round the jungle-clad hills in their eternal quest for prey.

The train reached the highest point at La Raya, 14,153 feet above sea level, but before I knew this—it was not a case of auto-suggestion—I had been attacked by the sirochi which makes the strongest man feel like a child. I took tablets and sniffed oxygen through my mask from the Cellophane container. I had forced on me guaranteed remedies of the guard, one of the cleaners and a very fussy Bolivian spinster. Most people seemed to carry entire chemists' shops about with them. Around La Raya was the watershed. Water sweeps one way to Titicaca, or the Pacific, the other into the tributaries of the Amazon to reach the Atlantic. Thermal springs steamed out of meadows of lush grass against a backcloth of picturesque, snow-capped peaks that glistened in the sun. Further on, at Aguas Calientes, pools of crystal-clear water steamed at boiling point in the ice-cold air. There were ever more signs, in the dress and appearance of the people, in the shape of their drab adobe houses and in ruins by the wayside, that we were getting deeper into the ancient place where the Incas reigned supreme. Near the village of San Pedro the first impressive Inca ruins appeared in the form of the Temple of Viracocha.

Further on the Vilcanota river (or the Wilkamayu), known as the sacred river of the Incas, plunged into the Urubamba canyon to add a contribution to its surpassing beauty. As the train rushed on through the countryside the roar of the engine reverberating against the flat cliff walls of the mountain, I felt no longer sick. Instead I was drunk with beauty. There are gracious hills and mountains, great rocks etched with veins of gold and purple, sheer cliffs out of which trees grow at right angles, and huge cacti which lift their long blue-grey fingers to spike an azure sky.

Nearing Cuzco, I looked into the great hammock-like valley in which nestled the square, white houses of 80,000 pure-bred Indians and I tried to imagine what Manco Capac and his wife-sister, Ocllo, thought when they first caught sight of the place that was to be their home. They must have been delighted to see a green valley sheltered on every side by foothills with the Andes in the background. Towering now over the flat and often box-like houses were many colonial churches, monasteries and convents, most of them partly built of stone stolen from the sacred places of the Incas.

Cuzco, which is called the archaeological capital of South America, and is scheduled as a national monument, follows the same general plan as the old Inca city. Within its boundaries were the remains of many wonderful Inca and pre Incaic buildings, shrines and temples among them. The centre of it all, seen from any of the many vantage points, is the Cuzco square, Huancay

Pata, of Inca origin, in which I visualized the glorious pagan assemblies and the colourful Inca processions.

The square is haunted with memories of the human sacrifices, the executions, and mass slaughter by the Spaniards. The golden age of the Incas drew to an ignominious close in a blood bath which flooded the square. What remains of the Temple of the Sun is enough to evoke scenes of the glorious ceremonies that took place in and around it. It was easy to evoke visions of the processions led by the Inca, carried on a gold palanquin, dressed in gold garments made by the temple virgins, to worship in the gold inlaid shrine. It was also easy to imagine oneself present on one of the feast days, when the Incas brought the mummified corpses of their families from the Temple of the Sun and stood them in rows each side of the reigning Inca. The square subdued me whenever I walked in it. I never had a happy thought from one end of it to the other. I never visualized a happy scene— always they were scenes of violence, the execution of rebellious Incas, and the massacre and torture of Inca nobles by the Spanish bandits.

The university is built over the ruins of the old palace of Inca Huayna Capac. The church of La Compania stands on the resena of Amara Cancha, also part of the Huayna Capac palace. The cathedral with its twin, open belfries stands on the ancient palace of Viracocha. Santa Catalina, a convent, is built on the site of the Aclla Huasi, or the House of the Chosen Women, one of whom, my archaeological friend, Peta, claimed as a forbear. Wherever I looked I could see old Roman Catholic buildings, many of them erected by vandals who had arrogantly knocked down the shrines and palaces of what they regarded as pagan and in so doing deprived posterity of one of the wonders of the world. The church of Santo Domingo was even built on the stone walls of the Coricancha, or Inti Huasi, the Temple of the Sun. Stones from the Colcampata, the palace of Inca Manco Capac, had gone into its indifferent structure. Only a few Inca relics had escaped though later I was taken to the amazing walls of Hatunrumiyoc, with the twelve-angled stone, to find them intact.

A Roman Catholic priest who had travelled with the same small party in the next carriage to me became articulate for the first time for days when he beheld Cuzco from the hillside. It was as if an agnostic had suddenly seen heaven in all its traditional eighteenth-century glory. He had lived throughout a long journey for that moment. He had seen Arequipa, Chan Chan, Lima, Titi-caca, Puno, Huancayo and other places and said very little about them. Always he had wanted to know how far away was Cuzco and when would he be there. Soon the other members of the party referred to him in private as "Cuzco". According to scraps of information he had divulged to his companions he had left his native Ontario for the first time in his life merely to see Cuzco and had taken in the other places, which wearied him merely because they were on the itinerary of a package tour. Apparently he had seen a film lecture on Cuzco in his youth in a seminary and it had given him an obsessional interest in the Incas. When he found himself in a library he would at once consult the librarian and ask if they had a book on Cuzco. He had said with shame that several such officials had been insular enough not to know of the place, or of the Incas who had lived there.

"I had to see Cuzco if it was the last thing I did," he said rather pathetically.

The priest had been captivated by romantic stories of the Incas and their golden gardens, where even the birds, animals, flies and insects were of solid gold. Cuzco, with its great discs of gold that had represented the blazing sun in the great temples for which the metropolis was renowned, had had such gardens. Cuzco had also had secret hoards of gold, which the Incas hid from the plundering Spaniards. But the beauty of the Sacred City was lost on the new-comer. It was all he could do not to stagger about like a drunken man as soon as his feet touched terra firma, as I did on my erratic way to the Government State Hotel. Owing to the scarcity of oxygen at that altitude one is apt to feel giddy and light-headed as if one had taken a dozen glasses of whisky. Visitors are advised to travel to their hotel by taxi, certainly not to walk up the steep road from the airport, and to go to bed for at least three hours.

C

IX

The Sacred City

I HAD made arrangements in England to be met and escorted by an authoritative guide around this sacred city, which derives its name from the Quechua " cosco ", or navel. Unfortunately my cicerone had twisted his ankle on the University steps as he left a lecture. He apologized that he could not accompany me to the cities of the Inca temples and palaces because this would involve walking over difficult terrain and entail some climbing. If I could wait a few days his ankle would be better. If he used his foot too soon he might be lame for months. The guide was the best obtainable in the ancient city. He knew the history of the Incas. He was also a student of archaeology. I decided rather than lose him to change about my time-table. I had arranged first to visit remains of the Incas in Cuzco and then to visit regions of remarkable archaeological interest outside the city. I decided to go outside the city first so that the guide could rest his ankle in the car.

Sacsahuaman, a massive fortress which guards Cuzco, was obviously the place to start. This amazing structure, which stands on the plain of Chita high up in the northern outskirts of the city, is a third of a mile long and has three sixty-foot-high terraced walls of monolithic blocks. Some of them weigh up to a hundred tons and measure 17 feet by 10 feet. They could only have been moved I felt by a race of giants from another world. Each of the walls had been built according to a well advanced military technique in the days of the early Incas. The great blocks had been fitted together so perfectly without the use of mortar that it is not possible to insert even a razor blade, let alone the much quoted knife, between them. The blocks looked to me as if they had grown together over the centuries. Each block was, however, an entity, quite different in size and shape from the one next to it. As at

Tiahuanaco, the blocks had been brought in some mysterious way by the Incas from a far distant quarry despite that the wheel was unknown to them. They had no knowledge even of primitive cranes, winches, windlasses or pulleys. They did not even possess steel instruments. I stared at the huge walls and wondered how these prehistoric Indians were able to quarry, shape and transport such monstrous burdens which would have presented a problem to a modern builder with all his mechanical aids. I wondered how ordinary men without anything more than their own muscle and ingenuity could have lifted the bigger granite blocks to such heights and then erected them with such precise exactitude that they had remained solidly in place, defying earthquakes and sieges. They were today almost immovable. The fortress consisted of three series of defences. An esplanade opened in front of the fortress. Across it rose a massive carved natural rock out of which was cut, as if it had been wood, the throne on which successive Incas had sat when reviewing the troops. The parade ground could easily be identified. The broad steps which led to the throne from two sides had also been carved out of the living rock with infinite precision. Nearby was the Inca's bath and the *rodadero*, a slide to which the royal children repaired when the parades became wearisome.

If this fortress was all that the mysterious civilizations of the Incas had created it would be more than enough to indicate that they were truly remarkable. But, as I was later to discover, Sacsahuaman was insignificant compared with what I was to see at Machu Picchu, the " lost city of the Incas ", and at other more recently discovered buried cities in the Andes. There were other substantial remains. There was Kenoco where one could inspect beautiful carved rocks with underground places of worship; Tambo Machay, meaning " Solace Inn ", an Inca bathing resort with swimming pools, waterfalls, and galleries; Ollantaytambo, where there was another fortress of Inca origin; and Pisac, where there was a smaller fortress built of " Ashlar " stones and including the " Intihuatana ", or dial, which was " hitched " to the sun. Also at Pisac, which is the capital of the picturesque Calca district, there was held every Sunday morning a remarkable fair at which, because a church service preceded it, all the Indians wore their finest and most picturesque costumes. Probably to compensate me for the fact that he was able only to direct me from the car, always taken as near as possible to any site I visited, my guide talked incessantly and eruditely between one stop and another. Much of what he told me corroborated what Peta had said. In the end I had a pretty high opinion of that young woman.

When I first mentioned her name my guide said he had read about her work as an archaeologist.

" Yes," he said, " I've heard of her—Peta, as you call her. This is a remarkable woman. When she was a girl, about eighteen, and she was the very image of what an Inca noblewoman would be, some people at the university who were organizing an Indian pageant tried to persuade her to take the role of the sister-wife of Manco Capac, Mama Ocllo. She was too shy or too busy. In those days she used to wear her thick black hair in two twisted ropes that fell down her cheeks to the waist. She comes of a line, right down from a prominent member of the Chosen Women, maybe a consort of one of the Incas. Such Indians as she regard themselves above even the few full-blooded Spanish people who live here. I'm glad you found her ear ornament. I can imagine what the loss of such an heirloom would have meant to her family. The past is very precious to the Indians mainly because most of them have no future."

Remembering Manco Capac, he told me in a slightly different way what Peta had told me about the dynasty. I was to hear the story a dozen times, always with slight variations, some poetic, some factual, and I was to listen to them all with rapt attention. It was like hearing a passage from a Shakespeare play or the movement of a favourite symphony over and over again.

" Legends," he said, " philosophically are impractical things. If the Sun God had merely produced inanimate objects the great empire would not have arisen."

The Sun God created, however, two children and put them on one of the most inaccessible places in the world, the " Island of the Sun " on Lake Titicaca, by which I had come to Cuzco. Manco Capac and his sister-wife, Ocllo, left the island and set off to found an empire. As in some fairly tales, Manco Capac had not now a staff but a magic wand which guided the couple over hill and dale, along the difficult route by which I had come in the train: It was after much wandering that they arrived in the valley of Cuzco, flat and fertile as now. They knew they had reached the end of their quest because the magic staff sank deeply into the ground. The staff not only sank, it vanished completely.

Though Garcilaso de la Vega, son of an Inca and a Spaniard,

sets out this almost as a legend in his unreliable history of these strange people, Manco Capac is regarded in Cuzco as a father figure, the first of thirteen Incas who ruled over this, the most mysterious of all empires. Some people told me they regarded Manco Capac as semi-legendary and said it was possible that archaeologists would in time set at rest the minds of historians who still did not know in which category to place him. Though much has been learned about the Incas, much more is still to be discovered. " Lost cities ", hidden beneath the jungle for centuries, were still being discovered and they would throw a new light on the dynasty to add to that which was already known. It is so far determined that the Incas began to establish themselves in the Cuzco basin around the eleventh and twelfth century. According to what is known the first eight Inca emperors did not very much distinguish themselves. They remained in and around Cuzco and were joined by other Indians who also spoke Quechua. They built their city, and they fought off invasions of Chancas and Lupacas who were jealous of the growing community. According to some legends the Inca Empire began to grow in the reign of the second emperor, Inca Sinchi Roca. It did not show any sign of becoming a great force in the land, however, until the reign of Pachacuti Inca Yupanqui (1438-71). He was the first great emperor. Pachacuti, aggressive and ambitious, made the Incas a force to be reckoned with. He organized the social, military and political organization of the empire which during the time of the eight earlier emperors had been neglected. His conquests have been compared even to those of Alexander and Genghis Khan. The Incas became pre-eminent. Soon after Pachacuti was enthroned in 1438 he mobilized his forces at Cuzco and made known, through messengers, that he expected independent tribes thereabouts to pay homage to him or be conquered. To help them make up their minds he attacked forthwith several small tribes in the hills round the capital, the Ayamarca, the Cuyo, among them, and slaughtered all but the young and the old. He extended his area of operations in an ever widening circle, conquering the river valleys, the mountains and then the north in that order. After his earlier victories Pachacuti saw the error of slaughtering enemy troops. He therefore adopted a new policy of pacifying captured prisoners and incorporating them in his armies under one of their own leaders. In this way a vast army was built up which was out of all proportion to the population of Cuzco.

Many great men are succeeded by poor sons but this was not the case with Pachacuti. His son, Topa Inca Yupanqui (1471-93), continued the conquests of his father but at a faster pace, adding huge areas to his dominions. The two Incas, in four decades of militarism, acquired an area of over 300,000 square miles, from northern Equador to Central Chile comprising a coastline of some 3,000 miles. Some experts go so far as to say that Pachacuti and Topa take their places alongside Napoleon among the world's blood-thirsty maniacs. When Topa died in 1493 the empire stretched from the Equator to the river Maule in Chile and from the Pacific to the Amazon jungle. Its armies were powerful and practised in the guile of war. They were organized, as all imperial armies in history, with many " colonial contingents " commanded by their own officers who were loyal to the Inca. The conquered areas measured half a million square miles and were called " Four corners of the Earth ". Cuzco, centre of the empire, and of the world, was no mean city. It had been rebuilt according to an architectural plan drawn up for Pachacuti. It included the Temple of the Sun, a shrine and a mausoleum in which were kept the mummified bodies of the earlier Incas. There were also many palaces.

The basic social group of Cuzco was the *ayllu,* or clan, and this became the pattern for the empire. Each *ayllu* had its own defined tribal area, its own chief, its own common ancestor in mummified form, its own cult. All the *ayllu* fell into one of the four quarters of the empire, the governors of which met in council in Cuzco under the Inca, to whom they were always related. The council made the Inca empire the first welfare state, a pattern for this century. Land, the herds of llama on which transport largely depended, the gold and silver mines and other means of production, were nationalized. The economy was planned so that no one went short. There were no depressions and no booms. The masses were regimented and skilfully deprived of initiative or private enterprise as in Russia today.

X

Gold Fever

THE EMPIRE became one of the greatest planned societies the world ever knew up until the development of Soviet Russia. The dynasty was founded apparently on the backs of other earlier Peruvian civilizations, the Chavin, the Nazca-Paracas, the Mochica, the Classical Tiahuanaco, the Ica, the Chimu and others whose names and places of origin may yet be discovered. All of them in some degree were skilled in the art of weaving textiles, in architecture, sculpture, pottery and ceramics, as well as in the working of ornaments in gold and silver, bone and copper. The simple ear ornament belonging to Peta which had launched me on my journey may have belonged to the Incas or to one of the earlier cultures. It is the vagueness about this succession of cultures, and the relics they left behind them in graves in the sand and in the ruins of mouldering cities, that lent enchantment to the study of Peruvian history. What is certain is that the Andean Indian based his political structure four square on the community, as did Soviet Russia, and, later, the new State of Israel, at least among the pioneers of the Kibbutzim. The individual was committed to the community and it was only within the community that he could live. All the means of production, all the land, the mines and all the means of distribution, the herds of llama and alpaca, as well as all the crops, especially maize, and the many varieties of the potato, were at the disposal of the State. Production was distributed through the communities in return for work. The proletariate were subjected to careful planning. They were given allotted tasks in the use of communally-owned raw materials to be performed for the common good.

Society was organized on pyramidal form. The Inca was at the top and the regimented masses at the base. Ordinances, devised by Inti, the Sun-God, and handed down through his successive sons, the Incas, were enforced by the four governors, their judges and chieftains of the clans. There was no currency. Therefore there was no capitalism, no contracts, no private property and no profit. There was also no slavery. Agriculture was organized through collectives, such as the Soviets imagine that they invented five centuries later. Produce was stored in strategically sited barns by the government, and the excess was equitably shared out among the people. In this way the Incas avoided the ignominy of being caught short of provisions as a result of such calamities as earthquakes, pestilences or famines.

For a long time anthropologists were mystified by the fact that a people who had no written language and could not therefore be expected to keep records, were able to register births and deaths, to record the growth of population, the increase or decrease in grain, the amount due in taxes and the area of land available for various crops. Then a strange article which might have been a flywhisk or a whip for flagellation was discovered. This turned out to be a *quipu* which, in the Quechua language, means a knotted record. The *quipu* (specimens of which have recently been discovered in graves in the desert on the coast), is a length of rope from which hang a vast and variable number of pieces of string of various lengths, thicknesses and colour. All the strings are knotted at different distances and in different ways so as to afford the greatest possible permutation. The *quipus* also enabled initiated accountants of the Inca tax office to work out complicated quantitative sums by a reliable arithmetical system with decimals. It is thought possible there were as many facilities for addition and subtraction on the *quipu* as on the modern adding machine. It was certainly far more complicated and efficient than the much later *abacus* which the Russians seem to favour even in the Moscow Academy of Sciences. It is possible that knots tied in different ways represented tens, hundreds, and thousands to facilitate the enumeration of the population, and the ' taxes ' they owed reckoned in the form of labour.

One expert believed that the *quipu* had uses other than accountancy, connected with divination, some with the selection of propitious days for coronations and enthronements. It had been demonstrated how they could also be used for recording in a mnemonic manner personal accounts of national events so that they could be handed down from one generation to another.

Among the astonishing innovations of the Incas was a primitive system of 11-plus selection which was carried out among the boys to decide to what craft or profession they were best fitted. It did not matter at what distance from, or how inaccessible to Cuzco was the home of a promising boy. He might live on the fringe of the Amazon jungle or in the high Andes or even on the nearby unpopulated desert coast, but if he had passed the primitive intelligence tests to which he was submitted by the local *curaca* he was at once brought to Cuzco. After that it was up to the boy how far he advanced in the Inca household or in the civil service.

Girls were not required to be intelligent, only shapely and beautiful, which only goes to prove how little human nature has changed. Officials experienced in the finer points of feminine beauty travelled round the empire at regular intervals and selected, at the age of eleven, all those who showed promise. There was later a sub-division of the girls selected. The most entrancing were ear-marked as *acllacuna,* or Chosen women, and were sent to the earliest type of finishing schools in the provincial capitals, where they were taught to be charming, submissive and solicitous —the three R's of the glamour world. The finest girls were honoured by being chosen as concubines for the Inca and his brothers. Those who fell short of the stringent requirements became Virgins of the Sun and were sworn to permanent chastity, from which no one was likely to seduce them. A still lower grade became secondary wives for the nobles. Those who later developed more on intellectual than physical lines were drafted into the depots of the government devoted to weaving, music, singing, or even the study of ceramics.

Some boys and girls of about eleven years of age, and this not as punishment, were used in human sacrifice at Inca ceremonies in Cuzco. The children were considerably doped with stimulants so that they laughed and looked happy. Then at a moment when they were completely off their guard they were strangled. Gifts to the gods. Finally, the throats of the children were cut to provide sacrificial blood to daub on the mummies or effigies of the gods.

The population was regimented with skill and despatch. As in Russia in the early days no one was allowed to change his address or leave his work or to perform anti-social acts. There was no money and everyone was paid in kind according to what he needed. The loss of personal liberty and private enterprise was exchanged for economic and social security in the welfare state.

c*

The control exercised was as rigorous as any imposed by Stalin, despite that the Inca dictators were god-emperors and their nominal Senators members of the imperial family. The Inca aristocracy comprised a large class of nobles and priests who battened on the masses. The organization of collective farm lands anticipated the communal farms of Soviet Russia. The masses were required to perform an amount of work for the State, in the army, on the roads, or even in the dwellings of the nobles. There was no real democracy. The emperor was a despotic tribal god.

Under such organization in a period of less than four decades there developed from a small State centred on Cuzco, a vast empire composed of scores of foreign tribes and administered by an army of bureaucrats chosen mainly from blood relatives of the Incas. Some Peruvians compare the Inca Empire with that of Caesar and declare that when Columbus ' discovered ' America the Inca Empire extended for 2,300 miles along the Pacific coast of South America. It was called ' The Land of the Four Sections ' and was based on the worship of the Sun.

In 1533, the Children of the Sun, as these ancient Peruvians were called, had the devastating misfortune to be discovered, and overwhelmed by a gang of ruffianly Spaniards led by an adventurer named Francisco Pizarro, just as the Aztecs on the Mexican mainland had earlier, in 1519, met disaster at the hands of Cortez and his Spanish brigands. Both these robbers were as fanatically Catholic as they were cruel.* They sacked and looted and raped as if their very lives depended upon it and then announced that they had done the work of their Catholic god. The Spanish adventurers had for some time searched for a rumoured El Dorado, said to be tucked away in the mighty mountains of Peru, fabulously rich in gold and ruled over by god-kings, Andean Pharaohs. The single aim of the Spanish brigands was plunder and it was hidden under the mask of bringing enlightenment to backward peoples. Both were prepared to massacre all who stood in the way. Pizarro, with whom we are concerned, had an army of only a hundred and eighty men and twenty-seven horses and, therefore, had to rely on cunning and treachery to achieve his purpose. He thought the Incas of Peru were the guardians of the fabulous El Dorado he sought. He learned of their Temples of the Sun, lined with pure

---

* Probably the most cruel Roman Catholic priest from Spain was Friar Thomas de Torquemada, Prior of Segovia, who burnt alive at the stake in the name of his church no fewer that 8,800 people.

gold. He heard rumours of great palaces and harems crowded with gold ornaments. It was even said that beneath the sacred capital in the Andes the ground was thickly encrusted with pure Inca gold. The sun, which this strange community worshipped as the font of their dynasty, was represented by the Incas by great discs of gold—golden suns which one could not look at without being dazzled.

Pizarro collected all the heady rumours about the massive gold of the Incas. The greatest prize he sought was the gold disc of the main Temple of the Sun at Cuzco, the whereabouts of which is still a mystery. This great emblem hung on the western wall of the temple and was covered with emeralds and precious stones. These glittered as the gold glowed when the rays of the early morning sun fell upon the disc. It lit up the interior of the temple as efficiently as electric light: the reflection fell on the gold ornaments, the gold cornices, plaques and gold plate to be deflected into every nook and cranny. As the sun rose the light changed in its intensity and lustre and added to the mysteries of the service that then began. The sun's beams fell also on the gold chalices, vases, water vessels and other utensils used ritualistically by the priests. They fell also on the second greatest prize, the Golden Garden of the Sun, in which the finest artists over the period had added a tree, a flower, a bird, a shrub or an animal all wrought in gold. Each artist vied with the one whose work had last been added.

The temple and it precincts was a place of quiet and of indescribable beauty. In it the workmanship improved by example until it was impossible to fault it. The temple contained chapels, not to saints, as in some Christian churches, but to the moon, the stars, to the rainbow, to thunder and lightning, each of them representing their deity in some splendid and costly way. Such was the picture which Pizarro carried in his greedy and vicious mind as he launched his expedition of theft and murder, deceit and rape —gold, gold and more gold.

Garcilaso de la Vega, descendant of the eleventh Inca, and a contemporary of Peta's forbear, later described this aspect of Inca wealth. " The craftsmen," he wrote, " even reproduced the leaves and little plants that grow on the walls. They scattered about gold and silver lizards, butterflies, mice and snakes which were so lifelike that they gave the impression that they were moving. There were also birds set in the trees as if they were about to sing. The walls of the bath the Incas used were plated with gold leaf. Pipes were made of gold. Even the Temple of the Sun was molten gold instead of mortar." There were other treasures of which Vega (and the Spaniards) knew nothing. They were only discovered much later. Among the objects found were life-size maize cobs of pure gold and models of parrots. Mummies were buried with outsize golden masks which made the deceased subjects look as if they had come from another world.

Until Pizarro crossed into Peru and captured the Inca garrison at Tumbes when it was completely off its guard, there had been twelve Incas. The one then ruling, Atahuallpa (1532-3), was destined to be the last. The story of the treachery of Pizarro and his treatment of Atahuallpa (1532-3), the last of the universally recognized Incas, is a fair indication of the calibre of the Spanish invaders and of the wealth of this old civilization. Atahuallpa, who was captured by trickery, was offered his freedom by Pizarro if he paid a huge ransom in gold. Pizarro, to test his theory that a vast quantity of the precious metal was to be found in the Inca El Dorado, asked for as much gold as would fill the dungeon in which the Inca had been thrown, " at least to the height of the Inca's upstretched hand ". The Inca trusted Pizarro's word and agreed. He sent out runners into the four corners of his empire and ordered his subjects to bring to him all the gold they could gather so that he might go free. Pizarro gave his word of honour that he would keep his part of the bargain. Soon caravans of llamas began to converge on Cajamarca where the dungeon was situated carrying loads of the most precious gold ornaments, the work of generations of the greatest Inca artists. There were all kinds of elaborate gold ornaments, gold plate, statuary, goblets as well as every type of religious object used in ritual worship and in decoration. It is said to have taken from spring to summer of 1533 for all the gold to be assembled, until the Inca could not reach above the level of it. Each llama had carried over a hundred pounds weight of gold, and had travelled long distances at the rate of ten miles a day. So many llamas arrived with their precious burdens in Cajamarca that the animals were said to have been tethered in rows all along the narrow roads while their owners stacked the gold in the dungeon. The total amount brought is estimated to have been worth £10,000,000. Pizarro agreed that the Inca had provided the ransom and then went back on his word. He had had, in fact, no intention of setting Atahuallpa free. A frightful carnage began. Over 1,000 of the Inca nobles were cut to pieces within an hour although they were defenceless. The place flowed with blood. The Inca was carried away over the bleeding bodies of his faithful followers to be tried for his life. All kinds of trumped up charges were brought against him at his trial which was a travesty of justice. There was never any doubt as to the verdict. The Spaniards wanted the Inca out of the way so that they could continue to gather the gold in the homes of the nobles, in the temples and palaces and in the El Dorado they felt lay in some remote backwater. The Inca was condemned to die in the cruel manner laid down by the Inquisition and the Spaniards began forthwith to stack wood for a bonfire in the public square at Cajamarca while other Spaniards gathered around to see the fun. Just as the Spaniards were preparing the Inca for his public burning the Roman Catholic priests, who had concurred in the death sentence, offered to reduce the sentence to one more merciful if the emperor agreed to embrace the Catholic religion. The Inca had a dread of being burnt alive and agreed. The priests at once went through the pantomime of baptizing the Inca, a ceremony which had also been practised in his religion long before anyone in Peru had heard of Jesus Christ, and then handed him over to the soldiers to be garrotted.*

The Spaniards melted down into bars all the gold they had collected as ransom and all the gold they stole in various parts of the empire. Gold that had been cold-hammered into sheets the thickness of cardboard for the manufacture of mummy masks; paper-thin gold made for pendants to hang on the temple walls; embossed sheet gold known as *la repousee*, some of it carried out in bas relief; and gold in the form of scrolls, the edges brought

---

* The Peruvian who told me about the execution of Atahuallpa showed me a cutting from a newspaper in which it was stated that the Spanish nation today still used the same method of execution as that used on the Inca to execute opponents of Dictator Franco. At dawn a few weeks before in the yard of a Madrid prison two youths, Gata and Martinez, had been garrotted. The youths had been made to sit down, strapped, in seats attached to posts, as was the Inca. Then the executioners came up from behind. The only difference in the method was that the youths had iron collars fitted to their necks instead of cords. The executioner turned thick screws with five pointed ends through a threaded hole in the collar until it began to plough its way through the living tissues of the neck. Then, after a few minutes, it snapped the spinal cord. The youths, it was said, screamed like maniacs. This most merciless means of execution is reserved today for convicted opponents of Franco, but long centuries ago it was considered fit for a king.

together and perfectly welded, all were completely lost to the
world. It took a conscripted force of Inca goldsmiths a month to
destroy all the hundreds of ornaments, the expression of the
genius of Inca goldsmiths over several generations. Some ten
forges blazed day and night as the work went on and as the gold
bars were stacked ready for transport to Spain. Just as only a few
negligible pieces of sixteenth-century Mexican craftsmanship
(and one great building) survived the vandalism of Cortez so did
only a few gold ornaments of the Inca Empire survive Pizarro.

The Spaniards had been interested only in acquiring gold and
shipping it back to the Spanish court, hiding what they could for
their own enrichment. They had been too ignorant to appreciate
the art of what they destroyed. A mountain of wonderful ornaments ranging from large Mixtec pendants to great discs of gold
representing the Inca-worshipping sun, were melted into bars
without a second's thought for the unique designs and the marvellous shapes worked with such superb craftsmanship by the
greatest artists in the world. According to Spanish-Inca writers
the emperors had sat during ceremonies on a stool of solid gold
mounted on a great square platform of gold. All the drinking
vessels the Incas and their nobles had used had been of gold,
worked with beautiful designs. The walls of the temples were
covered with gold and silver. The Coricancha, or the Great
Temple of the Sun in Cuzco, was the repository for a fabulous
collection of gold plate. The smaller temples scattered about the
empire glittered with gold. If the walls were not plated with it
they were decorated with religious regalia in which gold formed
the greater part.

One of the Inca nobles who escaped the massacre hid himself
among the peasants and saw how Pizarro set about being the new
master of Peru, and how his men took over the imperial capital of
Cuzco and exploited its treasures. When the opportunity presented
itself he escaped in disguise with a herd of llamas. The Inca
Empire was vast and the Spaniards had not moved far from
Cuzco, mainly because the thieves had fallen out, as thieves
will.

Pizarro and Almagro had both claimed Cuzco as their own and
had begun to fight each other. The noble reached Inca strongholds where he made it known what had happened. Pizarro had
made another Inca noble, a collaborator, the new Inca under the
name of Manco II, having murdered Atahuallpa and taken his

ransom. Thousands of Atahuallpa's faithful subjects were even then on their way from remote parts of the empire, where they had but recently heard of the emperor's appeal for the ransom, and when they heard of Pizarro's treachery they quickly turned about. Fearing that they might be overtaken they hid the gold they carried anywhere they could. There is no doubt that, for this reason alone, sizeable hoards of gold are hidden in many parts of Peru, in lakes or rivers, in the mountains, even buried in the coastal sands and in the jungle. It is the realization of this, together with the frequent discovery right up to 1965 of the location of a succession of buried Inca cities, that has given the country the reputation of having buried treasure. Many people think that some fabulous El Dorado is still to be discovered, as Machu Picchu was discovered, in the vast and unexplored areas of the country. It was at one time thought that this place might be where Manco II eventually fled when he fell foul of Pizarro, taking with him much of the Inca treasure and most of the Inca household. At first Manco II was thought to have lived at the mountain stronghold, Machu Picchu, discovered by Hiram Bingham, an American archaeologist, in 1911, and later at another mountain stronghold, recently found by another American archaeologist named Gene Savoy, and called Vilcapampa.

But still the search goes on, sometimes in a blaze of romantic publicity but more often secretly, in remote fastnesses of the Peruvian jungle and along the Amazon, inhabited only by small unfriendly tribes of forest Indians. There is little doubt that the Indians share the belief of the white man that some fabulous El Dorado exists. Some of them have even said that they have seen it, but that it is protected by spirits of their ancestors, and that if they told a stranger of its whereabouts they would be struck dead. When explorers have contacted some Indians they have said that the El Dorado is further on, this way or that, but refuse to act as guide no matter what inducement is offered. The El Dorado has always been a little further on than where the explorers were and in this way many brave men have been lured to their death. Either they have been lost and have died of starvation, or they have sunken in the treacherous swamps or they have been killed by the hostile Indians, some of whom shoot white men on sight as they shoot leopard.

The stories of the perpetual search for the South American El Dorado would make a book. On my first night in Cuzco I was told the enthralling story of a youth who lost his way in some underground working and eventually reached a clearing that was stacked with all kinds of gold treasure. He filled his pockets and carried as much as he could and then tried to find his way back. When he reached the surface in the old quarter of the imperial city the people quickly gathered around him and listened to his amazing story, to which his discovered treasure gave ample verisimilitude. One British expedition in 1939 spent £15,000 trying to drain a lake in the Andes that had the reputation of being one of the Inca hiding places when part of the ransom was jettisoned. Other expeditions had tried to locate some of the old mines from which the early Incas obtained their gold, just as men have tried to find King Solomon's mines. A senior member of one of the expeditions became detached from the rest while looking for water. He was not seen again for a week in spite of a continual search for him. When he staggered one morning into the camp, emaciated and hysterical, he told how, while lost, he had come across a magnificent city covering a wide clearing in the jungle. He swore on the Bible as he lay dying that the city was glittering with gold and precious stones. After the man had been buried the party systematically searched the area for weeks in the hope of finding the place but without success. A doctor who accompanied the party thought that the story was founded on delusions but no one else shared this view. They all believed that in some unaccountable way their colleague had found the El Dorado everyone sought.

Only two months before I arrived in Peru still another " lost city of the Incas " was discovered by a group of migrant farmers on the fringes of northern Peru. Having heard the stories of the treasure, they had banded together and ridden for six days without seeing anyone but a few stray tribes of Indians who quickly dispersed. Most of them were armed with bows and arrows but they seemed to be aware that the white man on horseback was invincible, a story that survived among the primitive peoples from the days of Pizarro.

Late in 1965 a German-Peruvian expedition reported that they had discovered two spectacular buried Inca cities in the valley of the Sihuas. The larger of the two settlements was given the name Lluclla and it was said to contain great dwellings which were partly dug into the hillside. A building described as a palace was said to be full of pieces of sculpture.

I heard these and many other enthralling stories of the search for an El Dorado when I stayed one day with a community of Inca-descended Indians to the north of the Inca capital. One Indian described in detail, as some people in England describe a ghost they had seen, a city in ruins visible in the far distance from a great height. He had hurried in the direction of the city, and he had an acute sense of direction developed during an active life as a tracker in the jungle, but found no sight of it. He ridiculed the suggestion that he had seen a mirage, or that he had been tricked by the sun and the shadows cast by the trees. So deeply embedded in the human mind is the lust for gold that many a man would have gone into the jungle to pursue this will-o'-the-wisp vision of untold riches. All I could do, for I was exhausted, was to go back to the government State hotel in Cuzco and repair to bed.

I shall never forget that night. Despite my fatigue, sleep escaped me. The air was bitterly cold but I had fortified myself against that by draining my whisky flask, by retaining in bed all my underclothes, and by piling on the bed all the spare blankets I could find. But it was not the cold that kept me awake, rather an overworked imagination. Some of the Indians, speaking through my interpreter, had told me evocative stories and I almost felt as I lay in the pitch dark that I was back in the golden world of the Incas. It only needed a little enterprise, I told myself, to find the much sought El Dorado. It was my intention to go from Cuzco to Machu Picchu, " the lost city of the Incas " which stood on " an almost inaccessible mountain " over the Urubamba canyon, called the Sacred Valley of the Incas. I also intended to go on to Vilcapampa, another, recently discovered " lost city ". Certainly, I told myself, there might be gold hidden there. Then I was to go from this romantic place, undiscovered by the Spaniards and lost to the world until last year, into the Peruvian Amazon area. Here I was to visit Indians in the jungle where nature had magnified everything so that all was absurdly immense and riotously exotic. Where there were deep virgin jungle, towering aboriginal forests, many-hued orchids, brilliantly coloured birds, strange wild animals and the greatest river in the world, at places six miles wide. Surely if anyone had wanted to hide gold this would be the place to choose. My mind roamed from Titicaca where the copper-coloured Quechua Indians herded their llamas over the tree-less tundra to Cuzco, then to Machu Picchu, where all the natives would be of pure Inca descent, and then into the virgin

jungle to hack my way with a machete through the densest undergrowth in the world, infested by poisonous snakes. As I dozed
off, the one book which had stirred my imagination about South
America as a boy began to haunt me. It was Conan Doyle's *The
Lost World*. I heard again, as I was falling asleep, the scream of
the pterodactyls and the roar of the dinosaurs which haunted his
Mount Roraima. It did not seem that I had been asleep very long
before the bells of the cathedral across the square began to fill
my room with insistent melody.

XI

The Andean Today

I HAD already seen enough of the pitiable plight of the present-day descendants of the Incas in Bolivia and Peru to realize how, as the result of war, a race of once proud, competent and mighty people had degenerated to become the dregs of humanity. Maybe it would be appropriate, therefore, in Cuzco, while the reader has fresh in his mind, as I have in mine, all the great achievements of the vanished empire of the Andes to describe, in contrast, what their descendants are like today, how they live, what work they do and what are their prospects for the future. Peta and her husband and other descendants of the Incas who helped me, and for whom I have a profound respect, may think it wrong of me to use the misery of the Indians to provide a foil for the glory of their illustrious ancestors. My only excuse is that I merely wish to dramatize in this decline and fall the great evil of unjustified war, if one can use such a word to describe the contemptible attack of the Spaniards, and to show how the consequences of war can last for centuries. In doing this I must say that many Indians today have great qualities that are latent, inhibited by the fate that befell their forefathers, and that a few who have been given a chance to escape from the drudgery and ignorance that has engulfed them have reacted favourably. That chance has been given by the International Labour Office and other agencies of the United Nations, whose officials I saw in the most out-of-the-way places carrying out an elaborate programme to help the Indians.

These Indians, who live in the high plateau of the Andes and in the deep and lonely valleys of the Cordillera ranges at altitudes of up to 15,000 feet, as well as in the semi-tropical regions of the Amazon basin, number over 7,000,000. Most of them are as primitive as people anywhere in the world. They are illiterate, wretchedly poor and often physically weak. They live as slaves trying to win a livelihood from the rocky soil with the help of such early agricultural aids as are to be found elsewhere only in museums. Farm animals in Britain live infinitely better than do these Indians. Their grass-topped huts barely afford shelter from the bitter weather. In places I visited there are no schools and not even the children can speak, read or write the language of the nation to which they technically belong. Their only means of communication are in Quechua, Aymara, or Uru languages and so marked are the dialects that have been developed by some isolated communities that they have difficulty in understanding each other at times.

Thousands of these descendants of the Incas looked the image of the Incas of old, portrayed so perfectly on stirrup cups and other pottery which has been found buried in graves. Many of them lived near to ruined Inca cities, temples and other monuments of past grandeur and one had the feeling that their families had never moved but a few miles since the empire collapsed. They eked out a miserable existence at bare subsistence level. They lived in filthy, vermin-ridden huts and had no water or sanitation. They were nearly always hungry and numb with cold. They lacked the will, the ability, or the means to improve their lot and seemed, instead, to have slipped back each generation. Until the United Nations officials came they had no idea how to go about increasing the yield of the few crops they grew, crops which, so officials told me, had been better cultivated by the far-off Incas. They had no idea how to build a path, let alone a road, and would splash knee-deep through boggy land for years without attempting to drain it. They countered epidemics, which took heavy toll of young and old, by fantastic remedies suggested to them by their own witch doctors. They had a superstitious explanation for all that happened. They knew of nothing outside their own limited experience. Since no one ventured out of the valleys no one brought back new ideas. Some isolated groups admitted they did not know there had been a world war. They had never heard of television, telephones or the cinema though they had seen, and heard, machines which flew high overhead. The United Nations' officials worked patiently with little reward. The Indians seemed to be sunk in a stupor into which their ancestors had descended when the Inca ruling class had been dispersed. They had lost everything in a national tragedy that has no equal. They lost their emperor and god, their faith, their homes and their farms. They were driven from big communal centres which were highly organized and had to take refuge in the most inaccessible and inhospitable parts of the Cordillera and the High Plateau to prevent their womenfolk from being violated, to save themselves being sent into slavery in the mines, or on the great estates which had been stolen by the *conquistadores*. They also wanted to escape the awful atrocities of the kind Las Casas wrote about in *Brevísima relación de la Destruycion de las Indias occidentales*.

United Nations' medical teams told me how they had found the Indians suffering from economic and social degradation as well as from malnutrition and diseases of many kinds. The wives worked with the men in the fields and then slaved until it was too dark to see in the dingy mud huts they called home. The breadwinner sometimes mortgaged his entire working life to some Spanish profiteer for small sums needed to buy seeds. Families lived together with their animals in one crowded room and the air reeked with the smell of stale urine and excreta, animal and human. The whole family huddled together for warmth on animal skins on the hearth in the winter irrespective of sex. In high summer the harvest was reaped in a new crop of babies who died unless they were hardy. The children who survived seemed to inherit a communal parentage. The only heating came from blue fires made of dried llama dung and reeds. The only appointments were coarse, home-made stools, boulders and brushwood mats. Illumination came from tallow candles made from the fat of their animals rolled round reeds. Water came from springs and wells contaminated by animals, sometimes frozen for months on end.

Some of the adults and children innocently admitted to me that they did not take off all their clothes for months on end and did not wash even their hands and faces except on feast days. The children, many of whom looked like little gnomes, started to work at the same age Western children went to kindergarten. The 'religious' sense, deeply ingrained as in all primitive people, found satisfaction in the bits of magic of the Catholic Church, some of whose missionaries had distributed pictures and rosaries which were regarded with suspicious awe. Few of these tokens were publicly displayed because they angered the Indian sorcerers and healers.

Doctors told me that many of the children died from smallpox, which was endemic, or from whooping cough, tuberculosis or half a dozen dread parasitic diseases. Their diet was deficient in protein and fats. Even if they had a few domestic animals and birds, wild turkeys from the jungle they had tethered and tamed, or little black pigs or poultry, the meat, milk and eggs these produced were for sale, not for family consumption. The money obtained for them was badly needed to pay for seeds. The staple diet consisted of dried potatoes, barley, or cereals, all of which had been grown on the Altiplano for centuries. The climate was harsh, the winds fierce and bitter. Only root crops could be grown. In some sheltered places the villages grew coca, which everyone chewed regularly, men, women and children. The Indians did not have half the calcium they required, or two-thirds of the iron and vitamin B^1, or half of vitamin B^2, necessary for normal health.

From time to time I was told that improvements had been introduced, in accommodation, in irrigation, by the provision of fertilizers and tools, but I found it difficult to imagine that things could ever have been worse than when I saw them. The United Nations began their International Labour Organization programme in 1954 with as much faith and hope as cash. A regional office was established in Lima. Three ' project sites ' were established at Puno, on the Peruvian side of Titicaca, at Pillapi, near La Paz, in Bolivia and at Riobamba. Each base over the years had developed subsidiary bases in remoter communities and these, in turn, had sent out their own off-shoots into isolated valleys which few white men have ever seen. The circle had constantly widened even if the men and materials were thin on the ground. When I was in Peru an official told me proudly that nearly 2,000 miles separated the two most distant centres: I would have preferred the work to be more intensive than extensive. The United Nations had in places built excellent schools, health clinics, vocational training centres, and, recently, libraries for the nearly 20 per cent said to be now literate. Wells had been sunk, fertilizers found, roads and bridges built. Groups of Indians indigenous to the Altiplano had sometimes been transplanted in lower, warmer, more fertile, and less populated zones. One dedicated official who seemed to be living in a community told me that he found it difficult to describe his feelings when he first faced a crowd of Indians.

" For a moment," he said, " I studied this compact crowd and the countless faces that watched us attentively and I felt my strength fail me. They urged me to speak and I could not. I could not face these slaves of yesterday who stood hatless under the burning sun watching us. I looked at their faces, lit with humility and curiosity. And soon I fancied I could detect in them a little fear. In this relatively isolated region the submission of the Indians was more absolute than in the others we visited."

There were times when I met a group, probably no more than a dozen, of Indian peasants on a lonely road when neither of us could face the other: when neither spoke, nor smiled, but seemed only to quicken the pace to put between us as fast as possible as wide a distance as we could. We both felt as if we belonged to different worlds. We knew we could not communicate with each other on the same wavelength. God knows why, but I even felt guilty. I wanted to empty my pockets of cash, give it to them, yet I felt they would not rush to pick it up. They might even ignore me.

In a publication issued in 1964, I.L.O. stated that the multiform activities of the Andean Indian programme reached over 400,000 people, but this was a mere drop in the ocean. It went on to say:

> These figures may not be very great when considered in relation to the total Indian population, or to the total need. But the influence of the programme is by no means limited to the communities directly served. On the contrary, a way has been found to reach even more distant corners of the Andean highlands. The men on whom this complementary, but vital system, depends are voluntary workers known as ' social promoters '. Specially trained by the I.L.O., a social promoter belongs to his own community. It is through him that outside agencies can be interpreted and explained to the community.

I saw Indians in ' modernized ' Andean houses which, although they would have been seen as slums of the worst kind by Westerners, were regarded by the Indians with great pride. They beamed as they showed me refinements hitherto unknown to them such as a window with glass panes in it, a primitive stove on which they could cook food, and rough wood stools made in Chucuito workshops set up by the International Labour Organisation. The floors were of soil. There was no closet. The old stone oven and the adobe brick walls were rough and unmortared. Some had grass roofs but in others the grass had been replaced by tin. Some had metal beds with broken wire-mesh mattresses. Women who had never cooked before made soup from the most unlikely ingredients, and served it to their excited families. I saw family groups examining simple chain pumps designed by an I.L.O. expert to bring a permanent supply of pure water for the first time to a large village. They had been made at a cost of £5 by the Indians themselves in workshops staffed by artisans trained under the auspices of one of the United Nations' agencies of whom the I.L.O. acts as co-ordinator. The only pumps which had hitherto been obtainable had cost £35 and been out of the reach of even the richest Indian families. Other Indians for the first time in their lives kept chickens provided for them by the I.L.O. on repayment of small annual sums so that they would have food of a better protein content. I saw Indians who had been used to back-breaking toil in the ' fields ' from dawn to sunset using for the first time simple farm implements made by Indian trainees at a community centre for carpentry and the metal trades. One man had a wooden hoe which was Biblically primitive, yet he and his wife who had hitherto turned up the land to sow corn and potatoes with the oldest implements known to man—the bare hands— beamed with sophisticated pride and pleasure. Older Indians, who had been used to sitting on the floor, sat on chairs made at a carpentry course and laughed loudly at the experience. Indian youths at a course of training, who wore small masks to protect their lungs from wood dust, made doors, windows and simple furniture. These betrayed obvious flaws but they were accepted with pleasure by the peasants. In one advanced community centre Indian youth had demonstrated to them a motor car piston and connecting rod, elementary to western youths, yet to the Indians talismen of a modern world far away, from which they had been cut off all their lives. An old motor car, a Citroen, had been brought from some distant place to Chucuito on a wagon to teach auto mechanics to the men. Hands that had never touched a spanner clumsily tried to acquire the sure touch of the skilled fitter. Outside in the fields a family which possessed a wooden wheelbarrow thought they had already entered the main stream of modern life. As many Indian families as possible were taught hygiene and food production and shown how to take care of a house, how to cook, how to wash and feed children. All this was part of a programme to bring the descendants of the Incas back to the standard from which their ancestors had been driven so long ago by the Spaniards.

Whenever I saw them the Indian women all wore their grey bowler hats no matter what work they did, in or out of the house, and no matter how poor they were, or how badly dressed in other respects. While the older women favoured brown bowlers unmarried girls here all wore yellow ones which contrasted sharply with their thick, black hair. They wore hair down to the waist, whether for warmth or because of the lack of hairdressers, I do not know. Sometimes the hair was plaited into thick ropes.

The plight of the Indians, especially in isolated backwaters where the families seemed to be bigger, even the young girls making their annual contribution to the population, filled me with sadness. It was obvious that most of them lived by a near feudal system of land tenure. Over half of the arable land in one big area was in the possession of seven families of Spanish blood. The rest, poorer land, was owned by 120 smallholders. Most Indians who slaved from dawn to dusk on the land had no chance of ever owning a parcel of it. The government was trying to redistribute nearly 90 per cent of it. I met some peasants who had obtained land though President Belaunde. They were still in trouble because they now did not have the cash to buy seeds and fertilizers, or even to pay for transport to take produce to market. At least 5,000,000 Indians, who speak the language of their Inca ancestors, earn between £6 and £12 per family each year. Few of the young children are educated, none at all in the high Andes, where child slavery prevails. At least 1,000,000 Indians suffer from malnutrition and, in times of drought, as in 1956, many die of starvation in spite of the efforts of Point Four to help by sending corn, wheat and dried milk. According to the Indians little of the food sent to them is seen at the distribution centres. Thousands of tons had been allowed to go bad for want of transport on the quays where it had been disembarked. A vast quantity of the grain had been taken over by speculators who sold it in the towns at low prices. In one of the worst-hit centres of the famine nearly fifty tons of badly needed grain was stolen in the night from a warehouse. The doors had been ' inadvertently ' left unlocked. Some of the cavalry squadrons fed barley to their horses. America had sent the food free but the Peruvian government, apparently not knowing the Andean Indians never handled a coin of the realm—they lived on a barter system—laid it down that a nominal sum should be charged for the rations. The official idea was that free food might make the already indolent Indians less willing to work. The Americans agreed to the charge, providing the money obtained was used to finance much-needed public works. Point Four officials discovered later that the money realized by the sale of the food was used to build handsome villas, garages and flats. These were sold at less than cost to well-to-do white Peruvians. In Cuzco the government owned mills and charged the drought-relief officials five times as much to grind grain as they would have charged private owners.

Peru had begun, just before my visit, to recover from the malaise of its military government, but somehow the richest benefits of life did not get very far into the Andes despite that President Belaunde willed that the Indians should be helped. Indians to whom I talked said it was the birthright of the Inca-born Indians, real owners of the land, that they should work as owners, not as serfs. If they marched into a hacienda it did not mean that they were breaking the laws of God but that they were merely taking over what God had given to all the people. Many of the big landowners were Spaniards, or of Spanish descent, and they were in the country as a result of " a wicked invasion based on treachery ". Did I know how the Spaniards had repressed, tortured and enslaved the people? No? Then it was time I, and the rest of the people, found out.

The fact is there was no repression, as such, of the 7,000,000 Indians but it was still true that most of the land, and certainly all the best arable land, was owned by one million Peruvian whites, mostly of Spanish descent. Much was made of the proven fact that 1.4 per cent of the Peruvian population owned 82 per cent of the arable land. Those worst off were cut off from the outside world, isolated between the unscalable peaks of the high Andes to the west and the impenetrable jungles of the Amazon Basin. There were no ordinary roads open all the year by which the Indians could reach the cities.

Suggestions were made by members of the U.S. Peace Corps I met that they should at least try to begin to build roads in the hope others would join in when it became a practical proposition. The man had been supported by Co-operacion Popular, the Peruvian equivalent of the Peace Corps, the Voluntary Service Overseas organization and the United National Association of Great

Britain in other worthy projects. Such voluntary work required the most up-to-date and expensive mechanical gear as well as men used to the rigours of the climate. The first batch of the Peruvian Co-operacion Popular which went into the mountain-locked High Plateau some months before was not very success-ful. The students, descendants of the *conquistadores* who operated in the same area were instinctively suspected by the Inca-des-cended Indians. There were signs of animosity from the first moment the two peoples met. The often haughty students had learned the Quechua of the Inca Indians. They had been urged to adopt a sympathetic and humble manner, and to try to understand the plight in which the Indians found them-selves, a situation, so said the Indians, brought about by the *conquistadores*. Teams of half a dozen students who had lived in mud hut villages I came across found it difficult to realize that they and their hosts belonged to one and the same nation. The Co-operacion Popular had built thirty miles of roads as well as clinics and latrines. They had also built some thirty classrooms in which, at night, after long hours working out of doors, the students taught over 5,000 illiterate Indians to write Spanish. Medical students moved in and the general health of the Indians was the subject of careful scrutiny. Indians were given the first-ever smallpox vaccinations. Minor ailments were treated and cured.

What had been done was but a drop in the ocean, but news of the accomplishments spread through the forests and the jungles. Travellers noticed a more friendly attitude by the Indian to white men. Hitherto all white men had been regarded as ' Spaniards '—a term of abuse. Indians told me they had met compatriots of mine who had come to the country in 1963 as members of the V.S.O.— Voluntary Service Overseas. I gathered that they were boys who had left school that year, accompanied by technicians. They had fixed up domestic wiring in a barriadas named Comas where electric current was available. The young men could have found identical work in remoter parts of Wales but the journey out would not then have been so interesting. It did not trouble them that within a few miles of Comas, and other barriadas which were also helped, there were many very rich families with three and four motor cars, a yacht and a couple of villas at the seaside and in the country. True the volunteers helped people who were poor, living sometimes in temporary shacks, but Peru had a fabulously rich population which was said to be adept at

evading taxation and which gave little to charity even if it lavished
alms on the church. The church was inordinately rich as a result
of both humble and generous offerings of the people.

A striking indication of the remarkable continuity of life among
the Indians was to be seen in the Andes areas through which I
passed on my way to Machu Picchu. A United Nations agricultural expert showed me fields and terraced gardens in which all the
Indians from nearby hamlets were growing the same crops, neither
of which I had ever seen before. They were, the official said,
kanuhua and quinoa, which had been systematically farmed
throughout the days of the Inca empire. The plants had been
neglected after the empire broke up and the Indians had moved on
to other areas. For a long time little was heard of the vegetables
though they had been popular on Peruvian tables for 900 years.
If it is possible to talk of vegetables going out of fashion then
kanuhua and quinoa went out of fashion. They began to grow in
a wild state as self setters and were regarded as weeds. A generation grew up which had never tasted the vegetables although, if
they had been properly cultivated on a commercial scale, properly
packed and marketed, they could have made millions for the
farmers. When the experts of I.L.O. came along they knew that
the biggest problem they had to face was to feed the Indians,
better so that they would be able to resist the many ailments to
which they were heir. They extemporized in several ways. When
they began to look around for ways in which to improve yields of
existing crops grown, they found at least six cereals and tubers
which had once provided a nourishing diet for the Incas and were
now neglected to the point where they grew wild and were allowed
to rot in the ground. Officials of a United Nations' survey team
made a census of crops, whether wild or semi-wild, to see if new
strains could be developed which would be eaten by the Indian.
Kanuhua and quinoa were examined at the Experimental Agricultural Station at Patacamya on the Altiplano south-east of Lake
Titicaca and experts declared they were nourishing, palatable and
easy to prepare. Indians were invited to eat meals in which the
plants largely featured and more than half of the guests asked for
more kanuhua and quinoa.

Indian peasant farmers in many parts of Peru are now growing
vast acres of the two plants which have become almost as popular
as they were centuries ago. In some places where the United
Nations' experts have not visited the crops are now being grown,

harvested, prepared and cooked exactly as in the heyday of the empire.

Let us hope that continuity can be restored in other more important matters.

XII

Revolution and Religion

WHEN THE sun set and the biting wind blew down from the enclosing mountains I became conscious of a moral and physical change in Cuzco. The change was in the inscrutable faces of the Indians I met, in the thin air, in the atmosphere that surrounded the Inca ruins. Cuzco became an eerie place at twilight. The huddled town of flat-topped adobe houses became overshadowed by the many Spanish colonial churches, monastries and convents. The inhabitants became grim-faced, reticent and surreptitious. They no longer walked in the middle of the narrow streets or the squares but slunk in the shadows as if they were so many assassins going off in search of victims. If they sat in a coffee shop they looked like so many bundles of clothes, their necks sunken into great anonymous ponchos, their faces disguised by thick headgear with earflaps. They all seemed deep in thought, resentful of strangers. Cuzco looked a normal Andean town by day, as night wore on it became the conquered capital of a departed empire dominated by the alien faith imposed by invaders. I have seen many towns under siege, or military curfew, which were happier and more animated.

Cuzco, and a few other almost Indian towns, is different from those mainly Spanish. The racial composition of the national population is the result of intermixing, first as a result of the rape of Indian women from a tender age at the fall of the Incas by sex-tortured Spanish colonialists, and later, as the result of a further fusion of Spanish and other, later, immigrants with the indigenous Indians. The Spaniards raped every female they could lay hands on. They changed by their violations the ethnic quality of an entire race. Some 55 per cent of the people of Peru are meztinos, or half-castes and only 32 per cent are pure-blooded Indians.

In Cuzco, and a few other Indian places, the situation is very different from the rest of the country. The population of the old capital and its immediate surroundings is almost wholly Indian. The Indians are as proud of their Inca descent as white Peruvians are of their Spanish ancestry. I met Indians in Cuzco who despised Spaniards, not so much for the treachery of Pizarro, as for the treatment of the Inca women. The pure Indian, who still thinks of Cuzco as his imperial capital, thanks the Sun God that his ancestors escaped the ignominy of racial pollution. There is no colour bar in Peru but people who are not directly involved will tell you that social preference is first for the white, then for any combination of Spanish-Indian descent, down to the pure Indian or Negro. This obviously is not the opinion of the Indian. Indians with Nationalistic aspirations hate the word *cholo* which indicates a person of mixed blood. They prefer to half breeds, who are proud of their white blood, even the Chinese coolie labourers who were brought to Peru in the 1850's following the abolition of slavery to work on the sugar plantations, to dig guano, or to build the Central Railway. Such Indians as these form an explosive nucleus of the militant nationalist movement which aims to get rid of the Spanish overlords and change the government.

A white Peruvian told me that the Inca-descended Indian depended very much on the sun. Only the sun brought him to life, awoke his spirits. The sun was important to him not merely because it dispelled the glacial cold or that it was so essential to crops but because, deep down, the old Indian especially, felt that he was a child of the sun. The sun was the heavenly father. If for private and personal reasons the Indians went to church in Cuzco they still prayed in their secret hearts to the Inca gods. Some of them found solace in the superstitious ritual of the Catholic Church. They even found in that church some of the very same mysticism as was in their own. Some Catholic priests had found an astonishing similarity between the Inca religion and their own. Both churches employed confession. Both fixed penances of fasting and prayer. Both used water ritualistically. Both ascribed all evil to a devil.

The Catholic Church has tried hard to win converts from among the Indians as well as the Negroes. In each case they appealed to the primitive belief in magic, superstition and miracle working. There are as many miracles in South America as there are blackberries on English hedgerows in early autumn, miracles ascribed to statuary, to portraits, to buildings, to ' saints '. I happened to be in Peru in October, which the church has dedicated to one of the more successful ' miracles '. Every October there is a holiday of thirty days during what is called the ' purple month '. Pilgrims wear purple clothes, which the church makes by the million. The purple month, and all the money-making ceremonies connected with it—millions of huge candles are sold to be burned away in a fantastic forest of superstitious light—dates from the seventeenth century. A liberated slave, says the Catholic Church, painted a figure which he described as that of Jesus Christ, on the wall of a monastery with which he was connected. There was an earthquake which shattered some walls and left others standing. The wall on which the painting appeared did not fall. With the help of powerful propaganda the superstition was spread far and wide that this happened because of a miracle. Celebration of the ' miracle ' was held annually and called ' Lord of the Miracles '. The painting is now the centre of a fantastic cult and Catholics of all classes hysterically declare their belief in its magical powers. The painting itself is so far from being miraculous that it is slowly disintegrating, much to the concern of the Church, for which it is now the source of colossal revenue. To add to the attraction of the festival, during which three processions fill the streets headed by litters containing gaudy idols, bull and cock fights are held after church.

"Only the Inca-descended Indians, with their nationalistic leanings, remain aloof from this outright attempt to win their souls," a non-Catholic told me. "For them to be able to stand aside, be the odd men out, so to speak, shows that the Inca religion is great indeed."

The illiterate Indians were under the influence of unembodied or disembodied spirits. Their entire lives, from birth to death, were spent humouring, or propitiating some spirit. There were spirits present at birth, at marriage, during illnesses, at the season of sowing and reaping, and there were the ancestral spirits present at death, waiting to claim the souls of the departed, to relegate them into some demonic underworld if their owners had broken any of a long list of vetoes and prohibitions, or to carry them to the higher world where all was eternal happiness if their owners had conformed to the strict conventions.

The older people lived in a twilight world between Catholicism, which was now the religion of all the churches, and some half-remembered religion of which their parents had spoken. The missionaries had told them about Jesus Christ, the God of Love, but they could not reconcile Him with Pizarro and his Spanish comrades who had come in His name to Peru and changed the lives of the Indians so that those who had been mighty were now humble, those who had been chieftains were now servants, those who had owned rich land now had to work long hours on the land of other people for little reward. They tried to equate Christ with Viracocha, about whom the old people talked in such tones of reverence, but they could not. They identified Christ with white men, with another world afar off to which the Spaniards belonged. After all Viracocha had the same miraculous powers as Jesus was now said to have. He also could walk upon the water. The Incas had mistaken the Spaniards for the retinue of Viracocha when they invaded Peru with their big new animals and their shining armour, for they came from the sea whence he was said always to go away and return.

In addition to their belief in a whole army of spirits, the Indians were hemmed in by superstitions relating to inanimate objects, probably a relic from the days when their remote ancestors were animists. All kinds of unlikely objects became *huacas,* or holy shrines, and had to be treated with the utmost reverence. The *huacas* ranged from a heap of stones to a mountain, valley, a river and finally, to some man-made structure, a building maybe, or a bridge. When they approached such a place they left a gift, even if only a piece of discarded clothing or a pinch of coca leaves. One of the greatest *huacas* was the Plaza de Armas where now there were four Christian churches built on the sites of Inca shrines like the Temple of Viracocha and the Temple of the Serpents. Despite that such churches were fabulously decorated, with gold retables, rich murals, painted and bejewelled effigies, gold monstrances and ornate altars, the Indians still longed for the gold bedecked Inca temples of which they talked with great nostalgia.

Everything I had heard from United Nations' officials and nearly everything I had seen suggested to me that the Inca-descended Indians were poor ghosts of their ancestors. They seemed peaceful and easy-going, uninterested in their destiny. Only a few, nationalistically inclined, seemed discontented.

D

Because of this I was amazed to find as I approached Machu Picchu that the Indians there were not only conscious of the great past of their people but impatient to throw off the yoke of the landlords of Spanish descent. The hatred that had existed in the early days between the Incas and the *conquistadores*, and which lay dormant in other areas, as it had been acquiescent for centuries, had been revived by communist agitators.

Almost as great as the danger of starvation was the threat of revolution. The cheerful response of Indian families elsewhere to the United Nations' help misled for a long time people in towns that the Indians were docile and grateful. In many large villages where I paused to look at ruins I learned that the young men were actively preparing for the great day when they would free themselves. The President of Peru was obviously well aware of the movement. There had been many acts of lawlessness and he was trying to forestall the communists by redistributing land. One of the great troubles was land hunger. Secret revolutionary meetings were held in the open at night. Groups of youths left the villages at the week-end to attend manoeuvres, or even to take part in operations. Training manuals issued were based on the methods of fighting advocated by Che Guevara, then in Havana, who had spent some months in a Peruvian sanatorium. He had married a local girl.

It was obvious that the Indian irregulars, who have since carried out several big operations against the army, had a leader of the calibre of Grivas and a central committee which co-ordinated all efforts.

"We are half the population," an Indian told me, "yet we do not have a tithe of the wealth of the country. The Lima government has expropriated estates in the Sierra. It says 25,000 Indians have been given land. This is an exaggeration though the number would be insignificant. The government is spending £220,000,000 on a big road scheme but the money should have been spent on seeds, houses, tools, irrigation, things we need at once. If we have to wait long you will hear a big explosion, even in England."

Despite all the efforts made on their behalf, and they were insufficient, the Indians prepared for the day when they would resist the régime. Peru had had troubled times before. Democracy had been last stamped on by military jackboots in 1962. The people had replied in the only way they could in a police state. They had staged such pathetic demonstrations as mock funerals of democracy. They had laid wreaths on the statues of Peru's liberators. They had chanted ' Liberty ' in the main plazas where there are as many armed police and troops as there are pigeons. President Kennedy suspended diplomatic relations and economic aid after the gold-braided military junta overthrew the Presidency and suspended constitutional rights. General Ricardo Perez Godoy protested that what his junta had done was " a Peruvian solution to the problem of preserving democracy." Like others before him, the general tried to deny he was a Rightist dictator. He promised full Press freedom by June.

The Perez Godoy coup had been primarily against liberal Haya de la Torre who had won a narrow advantage in the presidential elections. The attempts to resist the military coup ended quickly. Constitutional government was for the time being dead. Whenever an effort was made by the U.S. government to prevent other generals in Latin America from overthrowing their legally elected governments American financiers howled like hungry wolves. The action was ' against business interests '. In Peru, where 800,000,000 dollars of American money were invested, business interests were clamorous.

There had already been many casualties on both sides in 1964 but there have been many more since. Recruits had been enlisted and efforts had been made to contact some of the thirty-three chief Indian tribes in the jungles of Peruvian Amazonia and to induce them to join in revolutionary activity. Some of the tribes who had never been seen since the Wycliffe Bible translators contacted them soon after Hilter's war had sent delegates to jungle town meetings.

In one ambush in 1965 nine Peruvian policemen were killed. Terror was caused in widely separated places by the planting of bombs in government buildings and hotels. A bomb was thrown into a debutantes' ball in Lima. Raids were made for the obvious purpose of stealing funds to purchase arms and ammunition. Over £5,000 was stolen from one bank.

If the Belaunde government was hesitant in 1964, as some newspapers declared, it lost no time in 1965 in countering the menace. No longer did government speakers in Senate debates refer to the guerrillas as bandits. By midsummer martial law had been proclaimed over most of the country. The death sentence was promulgated for a wide range of offences. Belaunde, who appointed a commission to investigate the spread of international communism, obtained evidence by almost McCarthy methods. The commission reported a hard core of at least 3,000 dedicated Communists, many of them trained in Cuba and Russia. That the government recognized the gravity of the situation was obvious when the local police were relieved of the task of internal security and the army was called in.

It seemed to me a revolution was almost as certain in Peru as it had been in Bolivia.

XIII

Lost City of the Incas

THE DISCOVERY in 1911 of Machu Picchu, " lost city of the Incas ", high up in the Andes, was one of the most exciting events in archaeology. It was even compared in importance with the discovery of the tomb of Tutankhamen. Indeed, it was almost as exciting.

A succession of persistent archaeologists and adventurers had searched a vast and perilous area for many years in the hope of finding a " lost city of a mighty Andean Empire ", which rose to be " as great as Caesar's " and which then quite unaccountably vanished. The search was based on mention of such a lost city of great magnificence in all Indian folk lore.

Archaeologists had searched the Peruvian Andes above Cuzco for months. They had scaled walls of sheer rock 2,000 feet high that rose sheerly out of a gouged out canyon. They had driven their way through dense rain forests. They had hacked their way through jungles infested by poisonous snakes. Some had died, fallen from a loose foothold, poisoned by snakes or drowned while trying to cross some raging torrent. Others had reached almost inaccessible heights, their feet bleeding, their flesh lacerated by thorns and briers, and then had found nothing. Still the rumours continued. One by one, the searchers found evidence on uninhabited shelves surrounded by the vast ice and snow clad peaks, of earlier men, of whom absolutely nothing was known. More and more took up a fevered search.

One of these men was Hiram Bingham, a serious-minded Latin-American history teacher from Yale (later a professor and a senator). With money he had saved by careful economy he made the trip to Peru, convinced startling discoveries were waiting to be made. He eventually met a Peruvian Indian, Melchor Arteaga, who impressed him with his reliability and good sense. He told Arteaga what he believed and asked for help. He suspected, as did other travellers, that the Indians knew more than they admitted about the ' lost city ', but that they refused to help foreigners to probe the secrets of their ancestors. The Indians, as he explained, were superstitious. They believed their gods would be revenged on them if they disturbed the peaceful sleep of their ancestors. Melchor decided to tell what he knew. As they sat round a camp fire one night he told Bingham that on a shelf stretched from one misty peak to another, one called Machu Picchu the other Huayna Picchu, there was an Inca city which had laid undisturbed by man for centuries. It had been, he said, one of the most amazing cities in the world. It remained in its remarkable state of semi-preservation, a magnificent abandoned fortress, unvisited by animal or man over the ages not only because it was so remote, almost inaccessible, but because living things all seemed to fight shy of going there. No one knew who had lived there or where they had gone.

It is significant that when Hiram Bingham set off next morning to try to reach Machu Picchu Melchor Arteaga did not go with him. He probably stayed behind because other Indians would have had vengeance on him. There have been many speculations as to how Bingham managed on so difficult a journey without a guide.

Just before I arrived in Peru a newspaper explained that after Bingham had gone off without Melchor he met a small Indian boy who guided him to the ' lost city '. All kinds of Peruvian authorities immediately questioned the truth of this statement. Many wrote to the newspaper telling what they had heard or knew about the discovery. A controversy sprang up. Later, the statement was repeated in a usually reliable magazine, *Latin-American,* that Bingham had in fact been guided to the lost city by an Indian boy. Peruvians could not believe that the boy had ever existed. To settle the controversy the editor printed the words Bingham had written about the incident in a book in America*:

> Melchor Arteaga decided to rest and gossip with Richarte and Alvarez. They sent a small boy with me [Bingham] as a guide . . . Hardly had we left the hut and rounded the promontory than we were confronted with an unexpected sight, a great flight of beautifully constructed stone-faced terraces . . . However, there was nothing to be excited about. Similar flights of well made terraces are to be seen in Pisac and Ollontaytambo . . . So we patiently followed the little guide . . . Suddenly I found myself confronted

* Published by Atheneum, New York, 1963.

with the walls of ruined houses built of the finest quality of Inca
stonework . . . We scrambled along through the dense undergrowth
climbing over terrace walls and in bamboo thickets where our
guide found it easier going than I did . . . Suddenly, without any
warning, under a huge overhanging ledge, the boy showed me a
cave beautifully lined with the finest cut stone. It had evidently been
a Royal Mausoleum . . . On account of the beauty of the white
granite this structure surpassed in attractiveness the best Inca walls
in Cuzco which had caused visitors to marvel for four centuries . . .
I began to marvel that this wall and its temple . . . were as fine as
the finest stonework in the world. It fairly took my breath away.
What could this place be? Why had no one given us any idea of it?
Even Melchor Arteaga was only moderately interested and had no
appreciation of the importance of the ruins which Richarte and
Alvarez adopted for their little farm. Perhaps, after all, this was an
isolated small place which had escaped notice because it was inaccessible. Then the little boy urged us to climb up a steep hill over
what seemed to be a flight of stone steps. Surprise followed surprise
in bewildering succession . . . Suddenly we found ourselves standing
in front of the ruins of two of the finest and most interesting structures in ancient America.

Oscar Guzman Marquina, speaking in the Chamber of
Deputies of Peru, urged that an attempt be made to find the
boy mentioned, despite that he would then be sixty and his name
was not known. His act should not go unrewarded. The magazine
made inquiries. Though they did not locate the boy they were able
to state certain facts about him. A man named Albert Giesecke
stated that Bingham's exploration party went up even further than
2,000 feet altitude when " a small Indian boy with very black eyes
appeared on the landscape. He led them, a cutlass in his hand,
through the thickets. Then, from the distant centuries, an en-
chanted place called Machu Picchu of the Quechuas appeared."
Mr. Giesecke did not go on to say what took place after that.

My journey along the Urubamba valley to Machu Picchu was
full of interest. At small villages I saw ancient bus-trams running
on iron wheels on narrow gauge railway lines through primitive
streets. They were always noisy and crowded to suffocation.
Indians clung to the sides of them as if they were refugees fleeing
before the advancing enemy. The houses were built of rough
adobe bricks and thatched. Colourfully dressed Peruvian Indians
squatted on their haunches beside baskets of all sizes full of primitive wares, surrounded by children, pigs, donkeys and llamas.

During the whole journey I was rarely out of sight or sound of the river, a vast torrent of boiling water that threw up flecks of foam high into the air as it rushed at breakneck speed to join the Amazon. The Indians, fascinated by flowing water, see in the tributaries of the Amazon the means by which one day they will escape from their isolation and reach the sea, of which they speak in awe. I saw scores of them sitting on huge rocks over the water pretending to fish but merely staring as if mesmerized. Next to the sun the river meant everything to them. They jealously resisted the incursions of other Indians from distant hamlets who tried to build huts by the water. Beginning as tiny children the Indians had carried containers of river water to land where there were no irrigation ditches. There was a scarcity of land suitable for growing crops so they had made acres of terraced gardens, one above the other, on the hillsides, by carrying soil to lay over the rocks. They reminded me of the Aran islanders who made soil from seaweed on their barren outposts. They had the same deliberate, strong stride, the same infinite patience and the same slow smile.

In each village I saw the headman who told me how many people lived within his domain, what they did, what they grew, how many llamas they had. They always had something to say about the Incas. They knew the names and dates of the thirteen emperors as English children at school used to know the names and dates concerning English kings. They let me know that they wished the old days were back. I was always offered coca which I took out of politeness. I found it so stimulating and pleasant that I soon felt in danger of addiction.

The scenery was superb and I always politely drew attention to some dramatic feature only to be ignored. The Indians had always lived in the same spot, had seen nothing but mountains. They accepted them as the normal backcloth to their monotonous, unheroic existence. Drawing attention to a particularly lofty peak that was permanently snowbound and which had two smaller, even more graceful peaks at equal distances each side of it, I said through my interpreter that they reminded me of a bride and two bridesmaids, dressed from head to foot in white, before the altar. This highly amused the headman. He called out to someone and repeated my words. Apparently the first wedding for a year had taken place in the hamlet on the previous day. My innocent remark caused the population to think I was a seer!

Still we kept in sight of the river in the sacred valley of the

Urubamba. Now we saw little communities that had been founded by Manco II's officials who had fled from Cuzco. Brown-faced, thick-set men in striped ponchos and pantaloons that came only to the knees eyed me suspiciously: I felt, despite the progress of centuries, that successive generations of the Incas had kept look-out men posted at the approaches to their land, right down from the day when the Incas fled from the Spaniards.

At the end of a long bouncing journey through a deep, twisting gorge I saw in the distance the cliff walls of a mountain 2,000 feet higher than the rest. On top of it, I was told, was Machu Picchu, the place where a large body of the Inca refugees settled after their flight from the invaders. It was difficult to believe that right on the apex, on a not very wide ledge, was a city, the fabled ' lost city of the Incas '. The place was named Machu Picchu after one of two flanking mountains. It meant Old Peak. My guide assured me that there was sound evidence to believe that the original city was six thousand years old, a thousand years older than Babylon.

From the river, where there is a collection of small houses, we climbed a steep, twisting path to view Ollontaytambo, one of the great citadels that had commanded this approach to Machu Picchu. Ollontaytambo is the scene of a romantic love story that smacks of Rhineland mythology. The general after whom the fortress was named, Ollontay, had the temerity to fall in love with the black-eyed daughter of Inca Topa Yupanqui. Ollontay was of ordinary parentage; the girl of his choice destined to marry a man of high birth. Even their clandestine meetings, said to have taken place beside the river, were a grave violation of strict caste laws. They merited death to Ollontay. Whether true or not, Indian folklore has it that Inca Topa Yupanqui eventually allowed the couple to marry.

We were soon in the jungle. It was not possible to go far from the river, which still leapt on like some legendary runner, foaming and roaring round great white boulders as big as houses.

Just when the forest seemed thickest we came upon a clearing in which were huts of wood and stone with thatched roofs. Machu Picchu could be seen ahead. The valley deepened and narrowed and the river became more treacherous. Because explorers in canoes had been thrown out of them after colliding with rocks at speed the river hereabouts was called the obstacle race.

A track up the mountainside across a ledge might have been

D*

made as the final test of driving in the craziest of all motor-cycle rallys. It wound like a snake through the trees and at times became a series of suicidal zigzags. To add to the hazards, great outcrops of rocks bulged out like paunches over the valley. The higher we went the wider the vista. We paused, breathless, every few yards to stare in wonder at vast panoramas across the valley. When I looked below I felt the height sickness from which I had suffered on my way from Titicaca. The river from this giddy height was like a piece of silver thread dropped carelessly on a green carpet. The primitive houses looked like toy huts in a child's model landscape. Between where we stood and the river a condor flew, or rather glided slowly, and we looked down and examined its wide, outstretched wings, watched it turn and wheel about as it searched for prey. Just above I took some of my most satisfying landscape photographs, of a strange world of huge, perfectly rounded peaks, that rose symmetrically like so many pointed mammary glands over the jungle. Each protuberance was covered completely with green undergrowth of precisely the same shade and depth without the slightest sign of the soil in which it grew.

At last, breathless with exertion and wonder, we were at the top. The first thought that occurred to me was how a primitive people who did not know of the wheel could ever have come so far from Cuzco—a difficult journey by road even today of ninety-five miles in a north-westerly direction—and then have had the reserve energy, and imaginative insight, to cut their way through what must have been a dense virgin forest on the steep sides of a mountain to reach the incredible situation on the top of it.

"Don't forget," my guide said, "they would be carrying with them all the belongings they were able to save from Cuzco, including, so tradition says, gold ornaments of religious and dynastic significance to the weight of thousands of pounds. They are also thought to have carried precious textiles. All they had to help were the caravans of llamas. Each beast could carry only a hundred pounds."

As civilization has advanced on the impetus of successive inventions, accelerated in modern times by two world wars which extended human ingenuity as rarely before, man had obviously grown physically weaker, a pygmy in terms of strength and endurance compared with the giant of his ancestors. The lesson in this for the future would seem obvious. Human creatures were being rendered redundant by robots.

The guide took me to a vantage point, hinting on the way that I should not anticipate the scene. It was best to see the city first from one or two places only, to get a complete view instead of seeing the city in sections. The sight was enough to stop the heart beating. It was dramatic beyond belief, outside the comprehensions of the ordinary traveller. It was fit only for the eyes of people who lived on a perpetual diet of fairy stories or ghost stories. It was mystical and magical, bewitched and haunted. Even more: after so many centuries of neglect and decay, lost completely to a world that imagined it knew the answers to everything, Machu Picchu challenged modern man with an insoluble enigma. What else could it have been in that grand solitude than the royal refuge of a race of god-like giants?

My eyes devoured the panorama greedily. I could only repeat that it was all fantastic, that the city was more suitable to the secret worship of a cult than to a human habitation. The only entrance to the city was by way of a narrow pass which could have been guarded by a platoon against a regiment.

Luckily, there were only a few custodians within the ruins. I had an unobstructed view of all its well-defined sectors, that set apart for agriculture, for the nobles, the aqueduct—a remarkable work of Inca ingenuity which enabled water to be carried and distributed at such heights—the military sector with a huge tower which is remarkable for its similarity to towers in European fortresses. I could also get an unhindered view of the Inca's palace, the temple, the large Sacred Plaza, the mysterious ' Three Windows ' spoken of in Inca legend, and the Intihuatana, or sundial, to which the priests hitched the sun at crucial times of the year when ignorant people feared that it might go away and never return. I counted in all forty-five masonry terraces, each a hundred yards long, which furrowed the brow of the green escarpment, as if they were lines on the puzzled face of an archaeologist. Each terrace was ten feet above the one below.

" Take your time," said my guide, but I did not need the exhortation. My eyes wandered slowly from temple to palace, from the garrison to the guard buildings, from the massive watch towers —these commanded a complete panorama of this world in the skies—to the scores of granite houses. They were seemingly complete but for the absence of their thatched roofs which might have been blown off the night before in a tornado born in those lofty mountains. If the master builders of today tried to build a copy

of this city on a similar site the shop stewards would surely call a
strike, for who could be expected to carry such vast blocks as are
seen in these buildings so high over tortuous switchback tracks,
flanked on one side by sheer cliffs of the mountain, and on the
other by precipitous and unguarded falls, into the abyss below?
It would have been too much to ask the builders of today to take
the tea round . . .

On the mountainside above the city it is possible to see the
terraces where the people of Machu Picchu cultivated corn and
potatoes so that the population could be self-sustaining. These
terraces had been overgrown by the ever-encroaching jungle when
they were discovered but now they have been cleared they appear
ready for next season's crop.

Who built this place of mystery? When did they build it?
Why did they build it? Where did its inhabitants go when they
left, in a great hurry by all accounts? And what was the real purpose of the strange-looking pillar of a sundial, the centre of ritual
and prayer in Quechua to the sun-worshipping Incas? Why was
it called ' hitching post of the sun '—Intihuatana? Many questions crowd the bewildered mind as one stares blankly at the
stupendous landscape. The fact is no one can answer all these
questions . . . yet. The place has not been properly excavated.

Machu Picchu, perched dizzily over a narrow canyon which
makes the Grand Canyon look like a hole in the road, rides over
the billowy white clouds on the convex-shaped ledge as near to the
sun as it can get. When, only half a century ago, Professor Bingham stumbled upon it while looking for a lost city of another name
he thought it was the very last refuge of the Incas, the place to
which the condemned civilization fled when the vandal Spaniards
captured Cuzco. He had heard for years a romantic legend, of a
lost fortress and sanctuary, an El Dorado up in the clouds above
the Urubamba Canyon, but when he saw it he could hardly trust
his eyes.

It has been proved not to be ' the last sanctuary of the Incas ',
for still another city had just been found in the nearby jungle that
has every appearance of having filled that function. In fact, since
Bingham's death ten years ago, several other ' lost Inca cities '
have been found in the jungles of Northern Peru, in the valley of
the Sihuas at Vilcapampa or Vilcabamba (Quechua and Spanish
versions of the same name) and, most recently, at Pataz, in the
region known as El Gran Pajaten. Each of these vast ruins are

mainly hidden by the jungle undergrowth but enough is visible
to show that they are large and belonged to cities with great
buildings, tombs, plazas, amphitheatres and palaces. Some corri-
dors burrow into the mountainsides.

I wandered round the temples, the watchtowers, the tombs,
the fountains, the aqueducts and the steep stairways that led to
one level after another of the city of the mountain kings and I
marvelled at the skill and ingenuity of the Incas. Naturally, where
information is scarce—the Incas had no written language and left
no records—speculation is rife, among the romantic as among the
academic visitors. According to the verdict of Bingham just before
he died Machu Picchu was in reality Tampu Tocco (Window
Tavern) of pre Inca legend, a mountain fortress which was first
inhabited by the kings of Amautas, a race of incredibly strong
mountain warriors which ruled the Andes from Cuzco for sixty-
three generations. The last ruler, Pachacuti VI, was killed by
savage Indians in the Amazon jungle. The various tribes of
Amautas split up and set out to find new fields to conquer. One
tribe, the Quechua, stayed on at Tampu Tocco while Cuzco
straggled on in obscurity and decay. Then the throne of the
Quechua was assumed by a great new king, Manco Capac, who
wanted to restore the glory of the Amautas régime at Cuzco. With
his family he moved there immediately to be acclaimed by the
people whom he restored to their former glory. He called himself
Inca and was the first ruler of the greatest power the continent
had ever known. The Inca maintained Tampu Tocco and built
there a curtain wall with three windows such as is to be seen
today in Machu Picchu. The fortress is said to have been the
impregnable stronghold for three tribes which in turn vanished.
No invader ever reached the fortress.

An American artist whom I found painting a picture of the
granite watchtower told me she thought Machu Picchu was a
citadel in which the Incas kept the most beautiful women of their
empire, the Chosen Women as they were called, probably for
breeding purposes.

" They were brought here out of the way of the Spaniards from
all over the empire," she said romantically. " The guards who
occupied these watchtowers commanding all approaches far down
and up the valley probably had instructions to kill the girls rather
than let them fall into the hands of the invaders."

To support this conjecture was the proven fact that 173

skeletons so far exhumed from the tombs of Machu Picchu no fewer than 150 skeletons were of females. Anatomists certified that the women, or girls, had possessed extraordinarily fine bone structure. There may never be an answer to this, as to another half a dozen mysteries.

It occurred to me that if such women had lived exclusively at Machu Picchu they would have left behind them far more of a mess in the form of cosmetics, beauty aids, hair pins, jewellery and other objects of personal adornment. If the women were of great beauty then the maxim would surely hold that the more beautiful woman is the more fastidiously she does her toilet and the greater the disarray about her.

Mr. J. Alden Mason, America's greatest anthropologist, with whom I had luncheon at Machu Picchu, expressed the opinion after touring the site that the inhabitants might have been wiped out in a short time by a sudden epidemic.

He did not express the belief, to which some of his colleagues subscribed, that the Incas developed on the backs of a succession of earlier civilizations that had flowered before them. Nor did he say that the Incas might have been a continuation of a line of Andean Pharaohs that began in the dim mists of pre history on the Altiplano.

One of the most astonishing theories I heard from archaeologists who accompanied Alden Mason was that the Incas who remained after the Spanish invasion might have stolen away from Peru and gone to Polynesia on Kon-tiki-like rafts.

Whatever the truth, Machu Picchu to me is both a mystery and a marvel.

XIV

Servants of the Sun

VIEWED AT an unfrequented hour early in the morning before the sun has stained the enclosing peaks of the Andes, or at night before darkness has fallen, I found that Machu Picchu chilled my bones to the marrow as did once the reputedly haunted dungeon of a medieval castle at midnight. Every breath of the wind, every sigh in the undergrowth, every movement of a bird took on a superstitious significance. The ghosts of the mysterious empire of the Incas peopled the silent streets which climbed beside the deserted white granite buildings from the ceremonial heart of the sacred citadel to the lip of the valley. They were omnipresent beside the great sundial, to which, at the winter solstice, the sun was tied up, and at which all through the year people prayed. Mystery grew in leaps and bounds the longer I looked. The ghosts were astonishing. There were the god-emperors in their magnificent raiment, the Inca nobles, the vestmented priests, the armed warriors, the lovely virgins and the Chosen Women. To them all the sun meant everything. They saw every sunrise as a miracle of a new-born sun and every sunset as its death. They believed that the sun had human form and his face was represented in all the temples of the land by great discs of pure gold, rays and flames emanating from them. All the cosmic objects were religious symbols and they revolved round the sun. Cuychu was the rainbow. Catequil was thunder and lightning. Certain stars were pages or handmaids or protectoresses. Eclipses and occultations took on a mystic significance.

Hundreds of cultured farming terraces, made by an army of land workers who brought the soil all the way from the valley below, provided the population with potatoes which was the staple food. Stone aqueducts brought water from springs far up the mountain to convenient places where it was piped to a succession of fountains so that jars could be filled night and morning. Meat was obtained by hunting or by breeding guinea pigs.

How in heaven's name, I asked myself, as the day lightened and the sun lit the icy peaks of the mountains as if they were candles, could any normal race of men carry so many millions of tons of masonry, not to mention such huge boulders, up a steep mountain track? It had been all I could do to walk up it carrying nothing heavier than a pair of field glasses. It seemed for one ridiculous moment that the builders, and their materials, must have descended by some miraculous means from one of the planets, that these strange people were a race from Space as were the people around Titicaca. I examined even from a distance the careful stonework of the temples of the sun, shaped and positioned with loving care by believers. I scrutinized the rounded arched doorway and its trapezoidal windows that commanded wide supervisory views of the city. Nearby was the altar and what is called the Intihuatana, the sacred dial stone which threw its telling noon shadow among the temples—the hitching place for the sun. The priests, diviners, virgins, sacrificers, monks and Chosen Women, whose ghosts haunted these strange precincts, had all been regarded as personal servants of the sun, and reverenced as such. Their divinations and prophesies, their interpretations of dreams, their prayers for the sick, or the dead, and their services at confessions or at sacrificial sessions, all had been rewarded by payments of labour.

One novel idea I heard was that Machu Picchu could have been an Inca Vatican City, a holy city, and that the graves found were those of the Vestal virgins. Other graves, of monks and priests, may have been overlooked, may even yet be found since excavations are still to be carried out. But an Inca Vatican city would hardly have been built in an otherwise empty jungle, a jungle likely to be overrun by savage Indians from the Amazon forests. As the Peruvian government claims, the place might but recently (say 300 years back?) have been evacuated. It is the world's best preserved ancient city as it is one of the most baffling mysteries in the annals of Peruvian history. No one can say when, why, or how the place was evacuated. Certainly it was not the scene of battle but was left in time of peace. The closest examination of the stonework will not reveal any signs of violence, only of decay, and the ravages of time have been held at bay by the rich deep growth of the protecting jungle that wove a thick carpet over the place. As one walks, alone, as I did, out of sight or sound of any other person, the mystery of the city is oppressive. The imaginative person can so easily populate the houses, the temples, the streets. The men wore *huara*, or breechcloth, and slip-necked ponchos of various colours to which, on cold nights, was attached a mantle and a knitted cap with ear flaps. The women wore shawls fastened over the bosom with long silver pins, long woven belts, wound thrice around the waist, and veils hanging from ornate hats. Both sexes wore sandals of cloth, straw or leather, and ornaments of beads, rings, bracelets, hair combs. Ear-rings, like that of Peta, were commonplace. The houses had been thatched—many are today. One could see the slots in some of the stones into which the ends of the crossbeams were fitted to support the thatch; imagine the places to which prisoners were fastened before their trial or before being cast headlong as condemned convicts into the canyon; find round flat stones, polished by years of grinding, by which herbs had been pulped or mixed; and rollers by which grain was ground. There were also projecting spurs of masonry, the forerunners of hooks, on which ponchos, or caps, or even jugs might have been hung. The way the huge stones fitted perfectly together to keep out the rain and the wind incorporated all the present-day tricks of Welsh stone masons.

Like other clergy, the Inca priests turned mythology into what was called religion. They used methods handed down by earlier practitioners to persuade, coerce or frighten their followers to subscribe to the beliefs put forward and to give alms to keep the priesthood free from the necessity to work for their living. To give one example, the Inca priests exploited a superior knowledge of the movements of the sun. They knew the sun in June went further and still further north, that the shadows it cast lengthened, giving rise to the natural fear among ignorant people that it would escape, leave the country icy cold and barren, condemning the people (and this would have been the case), to long, lingering deaths. The priests also knew that towards the end of June, on June 21st or June 22nd, the sun would cease to move further north. They made it known, therefore, after gathering the masses of the people together that on this day the High Priest would tie up the runaway sun to the pillar of the Intihuatana. The people were duly impressed that the priests possessed such great powers. They expressed their wonder, delight and gratitude by slaving their hearts out to maintain the large priesthood in leisure in which they could continue to develop their occult powers. If the sun did not happen to shine at times when crops needed warmth because of mist or cloud the Incas who farmed the steep terraces called on the priests to intercede. People in agricultural areas in Britain until only a few years ago, before the B.B.C. weathermen showed how dependent the climate was on depressions and isobars, also called on the priests to ask the Lord to control the elements for their own local advantage. They forgot that if they had their way it might be to the disadvantage of people somewhere else.

XV

Last Refuge of the Incas

THE SECRET places where, according to old documents, the refugee Inca Manco II and his brothers, Sayri Tupac and Titu Cuci lived, were Vilcapampa, in Quechua 'late kingdom' or 'near a pampa,' and Uiticos, 'a hiding place'. As in the case of Machu Picchu, neither of these reputed 'lost cities' were discovered by the Spanish invaders although thousands of men searched for them for many years.

When Professor Bingham found Machu Picchu he actually thought he had found Vilcapampa for which he had been searching. He believed, in fact, that Machu Picchu was Vilcapampa. Some of his companions, and other experts, who examined the site of Machu Picchu expressed doubts that it was a royal city and believed that it had rather the composition, and the situation, of an Inca fortress, built on the ruins of a very much older city. Bingham was at first stubborn but he eventually formed the same opinion. He reluctantly declared that Machu Picchu was not the very last refuge of the Incas. Vilcapampa had still to be found.

Since the death of Bingham many archaeologists have tried to discover Vilcapampa and Uiticos, which are jointly referred to in old documents. An American archaeologist named Gene Savoy, a graduate of Portland University, and a native of Bellingham, Washington, went to Peru in 1957 to study the remains of the ancient Chimu kingdom, of which I shall write later. He chanced to meet a veteran explorer who had been working for some years for the Peruvian government clearing the snake-infested undergrowth that concealed most of the ruins at Machu Picchu. As they sat together in the evenings the veteran told Gene Savoy what he thought had happened to the Incas. Savoy, like all archaeologists, was baffled by the way the Incas, their nobles and officials and their reputedly vast harems of beautiful women, had apparently vanished into thin air. He listened to the old man's stories with rapt attention. Soon Savoy had decided to neglect the Chimu people in favour of the Incas.

In 1964 Gene Savoy and the veteran explorer decided to lead an expedition to search for Vilcapampa. The two men decided naturally to make for the Vilcapampa cordillera though it had been searched by scores of expeditions in vain. They went into the high puna country—the cordillera rises to 12,500 feet—because this type of landscape was favoured by the Incas. Savoy had also discovered that Hiram Bingham, before he discovered Machu Picchu, which satisfied his immediate aspirations, had actually explored part of the Vilcapampa area and there found some stone remains which should have aroused his interest but which did not. His guides, who were savage Indians, told him that the stones were all there were. Since Bingham had already half persuaded himself that the Incas would not have built a city in a region that was tropical he withdrew. Savoy had also learned that Bingham had said that he thought some ruins of horse-shoe shape on the opposite side of the river, but lower down from the Vilcapampa range, were probably Uiticos. Savoy had read somewhere that the legendary Alexander von Humbold had said that Titu Cusi hid at Uiticos and came up from there on a journey of three days duration to Vilcapampa. Uiticos was probably much lower down the mountain, Savoy thought, because Titu Cusi brought with him on the journey such provisions as would come from a more tropical region, monkey flesh, dressed macaws and venison. All he had to do, thought Savoy, was to find a narrow Inca track near the horse-shoe shaped ruins. He believed it would lead him in three days to Vilcapampa, ' the last refuge of the Incas '.

The expedition, which comprised eighty people, including seventy sturdy workers, acclimatized to the tropics and equipped with all the modern equipment for excavating rocky soil, set off with a caravan of mules. After many adventures, and some hardship, Gene Savoy discovered the narrow Inca track pretty well where he had suspected it might be. It led out of the vast Vilcapampa mountains, through a narrow pass at 12,000 feet, and then skirted snow-capped peaks for a long distance until the expedition came to a large tropical rain forest. The seventy workmen had to chop their way with machetes through a thick, matted, tropical area infested with snakes. After some days of hard work they made their way into the forest jungle and climbed to the crest of the Marcacocha-Piscacocha range.

As Bingham had found in his search for Vilcapampa, the native Indians dared not openly guide a white man to the sacred city. The Indians did reveal, however, that a ruined Inca city in or near the Vilcapampa range was known to the region as Espiritu-pampa, or Pampa of the Spirits. It was haunted with all the terrors that infested the minds of a backward people. The ghosts were omniscient spirits of departed Indian chiefs over the centuries. Death was the penalty for any Indian who betrayed the location of the city and the spirits would get the culprit no matter where he went. How, in spite of this, Savoy persuaded a few savage Indians to accompany him in his quest I do not know but several Indians went with him at least as far as the edge of the city. Here were some stones. They might have been the same stones which Bingham saw. At any rate the Indians said the same to Savoy as they had said to Bingham a generation before. There were no more stones but those he could see. It would be a waste of time to climb higher for they knew the area well and it was bereft of masonry. Savoy was too canny to be taken in. He pretended to give up. This satisfied the Indians, who went away. Then he began to work in earnest.

The party explored the vast site for twenty-two days during which, according to Savoy, the party discovered the separate groups of terraced ruins of palaces built of large granite blocks similar to those found at Machu Picchu. The palaces had their own water supply and fountains.

Some of them even had baths. Water still ran through the ruins on the lower pampa and the music of it was the only sound to be heard. Many pieces of ceramics found were identified by leading Lima archaeologists as Imperial Inca. Other evidence convinced Savoy and his experts that they had found Vilcapampa, the long-lost last refuge of Manco II, a mountain citadel of the first order. It was considered by all to be the most interesting and revealing of all known ruins of the Incas. The chain of pampas extended for about ten miles and the ruins comprised about two and a half square miles.

Savoy's discovery was heralded as of great importance. When Manco fled from Cuzco with his followers they took with them trains of llamas loaded with a great treasure, including it is thought, the great golden disc of the sun from the Imperial

Temple. Hopes were at once aroused that these treasures, and large supplies of precious textiles, would be found when the undergrowth could be moved to allow excavation. The ruins are far more extensive than was at first thought and while most experts agree they are part of the last refuge of the Incas, some are inclined to the theory that they may have been the original royal city of the dynasty before the founding of Cuzco.

Towards the end of 1964 it was stated by Savoy, together with his associates, Douglas Sharon, and Antonio Sanlander Cascelli of Cuzco, that they were organizing a further exploration of the area after the removal of the heavy cover of vegetation and trees which had grown over the site in the past four centuries. The task was rendered all the more hazardous because of the dense jungle growth and the presence of poisonous snakes.

Mr. Savoy later sent to Dr. Luis Valcarcel, President of the Patronato Nacionel de Arqueologia, whom I met at Lima, a preliminary report on the field exploration. In this he referred to recent field operations by the Andean Explorers' Club (which he founded) to make a general reconnaissance of the Vilcapampa area in the hope of locating the final refuge of Manco II and his three sons, Sayri Tupac, Titu Cusi and Amaru Tupac and Inca chiefs who rebelled against the Spaniards:

Our examination of the first pampa, known as Espiritupampa was detailed and comprehensive. I chose a section of six groups of ruins, plus a seventh for documentation for various reasons, mostly due to practical considerations—accessibility of the location, willingness of the men to work in this area and weather conditions. In total some ten other groups were studied, plus numerous small sites, which will be dealt with in my final report.

From the Preliminary plan of the Espiritupampa area and the Hispanic Palace in this zone (attached to the report), you will be able to distinguish the architectural characteristics, dimensions, to scale, and design of the ruins under study. My final report will deal with other areas included in our ground examination covering an area far more extensive than Espiritupampa (1,400 metres altitude). Our survey extended far up into the areas directly above Espiritupampa beneath the Marcacocha-Piscacocha range, into the zones bounded by the river Chontabamba and the unmapped river which I have named Manco II and its tributary, Tupac Amaru.

Gene Savoy saw that his examination of this archaeological zone was conducted from an historical rather than an archaeological point of view. He added: " In my opinion the site can be considered to be Vilcapampa Grande the final refuge of Manco II and his three sons." The evidence on which he based this judgement he gave as the extensive area of ruins covering many square kilometres; a minimum of four specimens and a maximum of ten, revealing Inca design and craftsmanship; the abundance of Inca pottery (fragments); Spanish colonial artifacts, horseshoe, colonial-type tile; the interrelationship of Inca and Spanish influence and above all its location in the mountains. All these things he said " indicate to me an archaeological site unique and unequalled in all Peru."

The Spanish-type tile, for example, with the unmistakable Inca influence, serpentine incision and red ceramic-type paint, would in his opinion appear to be conclusive proof that the site is late Inca. The fact it was removed from Spanish influence, or areas colonized by the Spanish, strongly suggested that the site was a refuge used by the last Incas caught up in the throes of a final struggle against the new conquerors. He went on to say:

My examination of the area revealed an abundance of tile littering the entire zone. My collection was taken from the Palacio Hispanico because of the superficial abundance of tile. But large amounts of this same material is in evidence in the general area. One has only to scratch the surface with a machete to uncover tile fragments. This is indicative that large groups of buildings at this site were roofed with tile, as opposed to the common thatch roof.

This finding would appear to be almost conclusive proof that the site in question was the final refuge of the last of the Incas. From historical records we know that this area was not colonized by the Spanish. The inhabitants of the area must have been Incas who had a knowledge of fabricating Spanish-type tile, possibly having learned this craft in Cuzco prior to their flight to Vilcapampa Grande or the tile must have been fabricated by the few Spaniards known to have collaborated with Manco II, or who were taken prisoner by the rebel Inca in his raids on Spanish supply trains between Lima and Cuzco.

The many excellent photographs Savoy took on the site included one of a worked stone doorway of white limestone which was part of an extensive area that had been cleared. Savoy waited for eighteen days for the light to fall upon the beautifully cut and

precisely filled stone blocks so that he could take a good photograph. He did not wait in vain for the pictures he took show the
sunlight falling right across the inside of the doorway and on the
approach to it. As Savoy pointed out, huge trees, some of them
measuring 200 feet in height, which had grown up on the site
after the city had been abandoned, had to be cut down to allow
the light to filter on to the door. There were larger stone walls of
the same kind of material. There was even better workmanship not
far away but it could not be exposed to the camera in time owing
to the presence of poisonous snakes and to the dense jungle growth
that covered it.

Bingham, who had visited the site and left without appreciating
what lay there said that from his superficial examination of Espiritupampa, " the site meets the requirements of the place called
Vilcapampa by the companions of Captain Garcia " and that " at
all events our investigation seemed to point to the probability of
this valley (Concevidayoc) having been an important part of the
domain of the last Incas." He was disturbed, however, by the fact
that according to Calanchia, Vilcapampa the Old " was the prin-
cipal and largest city in the neo-Inca state ".

Savoy's report continues:

> The archaeological remains are of a complex nature suggesting
> a city layout as opposed to isolated ruins. Since the plan includes
> only a portion of the one site known as Espiritupampa and since
> there are several sites in the general area (which I have named
> Vilcapampa Grande), it can be seen that the sites are extensive and
> suggest an interrelationship. We have, then, a very rich archaeo-
> logical sector hitherto unknown, except for those smaller sections
> examined by Bingham in the lower areas of Espiritupampa.

Savoy knew, because of his historical analysis of the site " that
chronicles of Calanchia and Ocampo indicate that the general area
of the last refuge of Manco and his sons points to the Espiritupampa area (though the area is in fact larger than the small site
known by this name)." By this he meant that archaeological
remains had been found to exist in the higher reaches of the Chontabamba river and its tributaries which flow out of the Marcacocha-Piscacocha chain and the lagoons native to this area—five
in number. As a result of the careful reading of the accounts which
mention Captain Garcia and his pursuit and capture of Tupac
Amaru—and a thorough knowledge of the area with which this

report specifically deals—many interesting facts, or what appear to be facts, come to light.

We know [said Savoy] that Titu Cusi built a residence down in the lower reaches of the montana, Pampaconas or Concevidayoc valley (Bingham believed he had examined this residence near Espiritupampa, at Erom boni Pampa). We also know that Captain Garcia in storming the fortress-strongholds of the Inca's refuge, had to pass over craggy heights surrounded by jungles. In my opinion neither Rosaspata or Machu Picchu meets the requirements of the descriptions recorded. In view of my recent findings the whole study of Viticos-Vilcapampa has been reopened. I believe this will add to our knowledge of the final days of the Incas.

Savoy said that if the President would examine the sketch plan he would note that Galpon del altar, a long structure measuring some sixty-five metres in length and a large stone (marked *piedra votiva*) which measured some nine by ten metres and seven metres high, some startling conclusions could be drawn.

It will be remembered [continued Savoy] that Bingham was particularly searching for a large, white rock near a stream and a " long house of the Sun ". He was aware of the large rock at Nusta Isspana at the time, but could not in his own words, locate another rock of this description nor a " long house ". There are other pertinent facts which add to our understanding of this hitherto unexplored zone. For example there are archaeological sites some two hard days or three regular days away from the lower Espiritupampa area, up towards the Marcacocha-Piscacocha chain. What are we to deduce from this information? To be sure, ever since Sr. Lopez Torres first reported existence of a city in this general area in 1902 (which caused Bingham to investigate the area in 1910) speculation has continued. But now we have factual evidence proving his claim. Just what site he reported on, as there are several, we do not know.

Savoy assured the President, based on his personal observations, that Espiritupampa and the largely unexplored adjoining areas were the site of the last refuge of the Incas. He said that the immediate question to be asked was how extensive were the ruins. He concludes:

Equally we must turn our attention to the possibility of valuable artifacts which may exist in the area. We know that the so-called

" lost Inca treasure " has not been found, the large golden sun disc taken from the temple of Cuzco by Manco II and guarded by the last Inca, Tupac Amaru. In addition to other treasure there is the golden chain of the Inca Huayna. If this treasure exists—and, according to historical records, it was not found—then we may speculate as to its whereabouts. Tupac Amaru might well have taken it with him when Garcia began his pursuit of this unfortunate Inca. On the other hand he may not have taken the treasure with him. As far as we know he did not have it when he was captured and taken to Cuzco for execution. If these objects exist they rightfully belong to the nation's museums.

The route followed by the party from Machu Picchu to the area of exploration at Espiritupampa was at first suitable for travelling by truck—from the start to S. Maria—and then the route degenerated and was only fit for mule transport along the Villabamba river past Plataybamba, Huayrurani, Lucma, Rosaspata and Pampaconas. The area was wild and mountainous but well watered by tributaries of several rivers.

There were other discoveries of ruins on the most unlikely places, one by a group of exploring farmers, but the next great sensation came again from Gene Savoy. In October, 1965 he returned from another exploration into the jungle area on the eastern slopes of the Central Cordillera near Pataz in the area known as the El Gran Pajaten to report that he had made another great discovery. In this jungle at a point nearly parallel with Trujillo on the coast Savoy found the remains of a stone city of about $92\frac{1}{2}$ square miles with well-defined roads. There were excellently built temples, the walls of which were decorated with anthropomorphic and zoomorphic gargoyle heads which bear a likeness to early Chavin culture. This culture extended over the northern Peruvian highlands and into some of the coastal valleys. The temples, however, suggest late Mayan architecture in Yucatan. The Peruvian Chavin culture according to *The Times* (25th October, 1965) reached its apogee between 100 and 800 B.C. while the earliest date so far discovered on a Mayan monument is A.D. 320 (Tikal) and most of the Yucatan structures were built several centuries later.

What was of particular interest was that the Incas fought with a northern tribe known as Chachapoyas. The town of Chachapoyas stands on a sharp loop of the Ucayali river, part of the Amazon about twenty-five miles from Kuelap and a hundred miles from Pajaten. It is thought that the ruins may be of the city that was built by this tribe. It has been proved that the god of the Chachapoyas was the condor. A condor in relief has been found on some of the walls.

Photographs brought back by the explorer show that the Pajaten ruins belong to a hitherto unknown civilization. The fortress of Kuelap, on a hill some way north of Pajaten was almost certainly built by the same people. Mr. Savoy says one of the roads leading out of Pajaten run in the general direction of Kuelap.

The Times in October, 1965, pointed out that Garcilasco de la Vega Inca in his Royal Commentaries says the Inca emperor, Tupac Yupanqui, during his campaigns of conquest in the mid-fifteenth century, fought many bitter battles with a northern tribe called the Chachapoyas, and eventually defeated them and forced them to retreat into the eastern jungles. Tupac Yupanqui was reported to have reached and taken the stronghold of this warrior people, although the chronicles differ as to whether he was able to hold it. The present-day town of Chachapoyas stands about thirty miles from Kuelap and a hundred miles from Pajaten and it may well be that the newly discovered city was built by this people, especially as a stylized condor appears in relief on some of the walls.

XVI

Missing Explorers

IN A jungle village in the sacred valley of the Incas beyond Machu Picchu I met a German-Peruvian team of explorers who were resting in camp until a woman member of the party had recovered from a severe chill caught high up in the Andes. I doubt if they would have invited me to eat with them if I had not been able to talk German. They were pleased to meet an Englishman, the author of a book they knew,* in so remote a place who could also converse with them in their own tongue. By their camp fire beside the river we talked for hours about the hidden mountain fortress known as Vilcapampa. They agreed that Machu Picchu, ' the lost city of the Incas ' was not Vilcapampa as the American archaeologist, Hiram Bingham, had declared. They also discounted similar claims made more recently for other ' lost cities ' discovered in the jungle.

The oldest member of the party, formerly a Panzer colonel in the Western Desert, asked me if I knew the story of Colonel Percy Harrison Fawcett, who, together with his son, Jack, and Mr. Raleigh Rimmell vanished while trying to find a legendary lost empire in the vast jungle of Amazonia. He told me that he knew Brian Fawcett, son of Colonel Fawcett, who had still not yet given up hope of finding his brother. " I met him on the liner *Andes* with his wife, Ruth," he said. " It would be in the late fifties, I think, and we were both coming on to Brazil. Brian was going to make a search by air over the unexplored jungle. I learned later out here, a year or two back, that people were still finding leaflets in English and Portuguese which Brian dropped from the aeroplane." The colonel opened a wallet and withdrew a tattered leaflet. " Here is one. You can read the English quite clearly."

The paper contained several questions addressed to " Jack

* Berlin Twilight (Hutchinson).

Fawcett ". Three of them were readable. They were: "Do you want to be brought out?" "Can you control the Indians if we land?" and "Is my father still alive?" Brian Fawcett had shown by the most ingenious sketches in the leaflet how a reply to the questions could be signalled to the aircraft on subsequent flights over the same route. If the answer was in the affirmative a second leaflet would be dropped. This would say, "We are going away now but we shall be returning as soon as an expedition can be organized." The colonel did not know whether any signalled recognition was received out of the jungle, although some 20,000 square miles was over flown on leaflet raids. He asked me if I could find out for him.

The colonel had given lectures in Germany and Scandinavia on the Fawcett case. He said that the Fawcett party originally went from Cuyaba to the Rio Kul Hiuene and then worked their way east. There was still much confusion as to where eventually Fawcett went. Travellers declared they saw him going north and south. Commander George Dyott, who took an expedition into the country of the Calapalos Indians to look for the lost explorers was told that they had camped in widely separated places as they had travelled through the jungle into the country of the Anauguas. Indian tribal scouts had seen the smoke of their camp fires. One old chief then said that he believed the Anauguas Indians had murdered the members of Fawcett's party. Later, another chief declared that the party had fallen foul of the fierce Suya Indians. Some ten different groups of explorers tried to find Fawcett but failed. Some of the stories they told were at complete variance with Fawcett's supposed route.

Many theories were developed and the colonel seemed to know them all. An article contributed by a New Zealand correspondent to *Light*, the psychic research journal, had, he said, published an astonishing claim that a message had been received from the lost explorers through a medium. The writer said that his sister, who was a clairaudient and clairvoyant, sent out strong thoughts to Colonel Fawcett. After a while the woman received communication which stated that Colonel Fawcett, his son Jack, and their companion, Raleigh Rimmell, all perished in the desert through lack of water. The medium declared that Fawcett had met a tribe of Indians unknown to white men who directed him to a 'city of forgotten people' on the other side of the desert. He and his companions reached the city which they found to be magnificently built with a huge temple which was lit by what they thought was a radio-active light. The dome of the temple was decorated with many symbolic figures which were reminiscent of ancient Egypt. In an open tomb on the outskirts of the city were embalmed figures lying in a row, their faces covered with gold masks. The figures were tall, with oval, handsome features and high cheek bones and they resembled the ancient Egyptians. Apparently the city showed signs of a high state of civilization. The stone of the buildings was polished and creamy. Utensils were mainly of gold. One of the strange features of these absurdities is that they draw from the little known claim that the Incas were influenced by ancient Egyptians.

It was further stated that on their way back from the city the explorers ran out of food and water and died. An Italian explorer, Alfredo Realini, told the Brazilian paper, *A Noite*, that he had seen the skeletons of three men and had heard stories of three men who passed through the Roncador mountains in search of ' a lost civilization '. He added that he had met a tribe of Indians, the chief of whom had told him that Colonel Fawcett had become his friend. The explorers, said the chief, had gone far into the thickest jungle and pitched camp with the help of three friendly Indians. Soon after they had settled in for the night a tribe of hostile Indians had appeared to discover who had lit a camp fire. The bodies of Fawcett and his companions were later found in a cave, he said. Signor Realini declared that he himself visited the cave and found in it three skeletons. He judged them, from the shape of the skulls, to belong to white men. The Royal Anthropological Institute stated in the fifties that the human remains which were brought to England were not those of Colonel Fawcett and his companions.

Three referees, Professor A. J. E. Cave, Professor of Anatomy at St. Bartholomew's Hospital Medical College, Miss A. M. Tildesley, former curator of Human Osteology at the Royal College of Surgeons' museum and Dr. J. C. Trevor, a Cambridge lecturer on anthropology, said that the upper jaw of the skeleton claimed to be that of Fawcett could not be his. The colonel's spare upper denture was available for comparison with the denture on the jaw of the skeleton. The two were completely dissimilar. The skeleton was of a man 5 feet 7 inches, Colonel Fawcett was 6 feet 2 inches. Just about the same time a report reached Britain that a Brazilian explorer, Willy Aureli, claimed he had seen

Colonel Fawcett alive in a remote Calapalos Indian village in 1948. He said that some twenty other white men were with Fawcett whose real headquarters were in a jungle village in the heart of the remote Xingu river area. He declared that Fawcett had assumed a position as one of the Calapalos Indian chiefs. Still later, in 1951, a Brazilian declared that Fawcett and his party had been killed by three young Indian warriors named Cuvicuiri, Aravo and Arrevirra. The three Indians had been beaten he said, by the chief of the Calapalos Indians because they had at first refused to guide Fawcett and his companions beyond tribal territory. When eventually the men were forced to act as guides they had taken their revenge and killed the Englishmen. Clues which persuaded Aureli that the facts were as stated included ' a nearly illegible inscription found near the place where the bones of the Englishmen were exhumed, a long jungle knife bearing a British trade mark and a boot.'

The German had investigated some thirty different stories with the intention of writing a book. He had spoken to a Roman Catholic missionary, Father Molloy, who claimed to have met a tribal chief called ' White god of the Sun '. This chief had told him Colonel Fawcett was alive. He had also met members of a U.S. expedition which went out to try to find Fawcett and failed. A Swiss trapper who camped on the borders of the Xingu had said he had met a bearded, blue-eyed white man held prisoner by the natives. He declared that the white man called himself ' colonel '.

Later a ' white savage ' was stated to have been found in the Brazilian jungle, but the colonel thought he was an albino found earlier by the missionary.

There were so many reports, all of them contradictory, said the German colonel, that Brian Fawcett, Colonel Fawcett's son, left Southampton in 1955 with his wife, Ruth, in the liner *Andes* to search by air the unexplored jungle over a vast area of Amazonas. Brian did not believe that his father was still alive, but thought there was a chance that his elder brother, Jack, could be. Brian covered a vast area, all of it unexplored. Explorers of various nationalities had gone into the jungle and some had never returned. Only a few rubber trappers had survived a deep penetration and they had said that a white man was living with a tribe deep in the interior. If Jack Fawcett is alive today he will be aged sixty-three and they thought he was much younger.

After leaving the German-Peruvian party I heard other stories about Fawcett from travellers who had visited Peru and Brazil every year since the first World War. None of them believed that Jack Fawcett was alive, not to mention his father. One explorer had been with Richard Mason days before he was murdered by Indians in September, 1961 while exploring tributaries of the Amazon.

" There are Indians in the jungle who are stark staring mad," one of them told me. " They would be scared stiff seeing a white man and they would waste no time in killing him. The story of what happened to the Incas at the hands of the Spaniards has been handed down by word of mouth and this has made many of the savage Indians suspicious of all white men."

It was hoped in 1965 that an expedition sent by the Central Brazilian Foundation to cross nearly 400 miles of unexplored jungle on the borders of the Mato Grosso and Para would probably hear something that would help solve the mystery of Colonel Fawcett in the area of the Xingu, one of the Amazon tributaries. They met many primitive people, forest Indians among them, who were living nomadic lives. A tribe of Crahiacoro Indians, who are seven feet tall, were stated to have attacked a post held by a team belonging to the Indian Protection Service. The chief of the Menkromotire tribe, who had also been attacked by the Crahia-coro, swore that they were a tribe of giants. He produced a number of captured bows which proved to an ergonomicalist that they could not have been used by men shorter than seven feet tall.

XVII

City of Kings

I WANTED next to go to the Amazon, the upper part of which, from its source to Iquitos in Peru, is called Maronon, and the rest, from Iquitos to the Atlantic in Brazil, Amazonas. I wanted to see something of the virgin equatorial forest that flanks this amazing river, the greatest in the world in the area of its drainage—2,722,000 square miles—and the greatest in the world in the volume of water it carries to the ocean. I wanted to meet some of the barbarous Peruvian forest Indians, and to see something of the amazing flora and fauna along the Amazon of which I had heard so much. If, on top of that, I could gather stories of ' lost cities ' or ' buried treasure ' such as had been circulating in this part of the world ever since Pizarro, all to the good.

I had met several Peruvians who had spent much time exploring the Amazon in Peru and Brazil. One of them had made the comparatively easy journey from Lima (1,000 miles) to Lake Lauricocha, the most northerly of a chain of glacier-fed lakes on the eastern border of the main range of the Andes in Central Peru. He had earned his living for a year lecturing on this lake, the source of the main stream. No one he said, had been along the whole course of the river, 4,000 miles long until lately. I heard from an American about the United States steamer, *Wilmington*, which ascended the river to Iquitos in 1899, an act generally thought to be dangerous, if not impossible. The average current of the river is five miles an hour but it travels during the rainy season at twelve miles an hour as it leaves the Peruvian plateau. The average depth in the rainy season is 120 feet but the flood levels at Iquitos can be very high. The river is from four to six miles wide at times and there are occasions when it divides into two main streams with inland lateral channels.

E

Some of the older Amazonian travellers, including an experienced Staffordshire commander, told me that the river was now neglected up from Iquitos, the very area on which I wanted to travel. This stretch had been first navigated in 1541 from the Andes to the sea by Orellana, Pizarro's lieutenant, to whom I earlier referred. He reached the main stream by way of the Napo river. It is thought the name Amazonas was given to the river by Orellano after his battle with Tapuyas savages directed (he believed) by 'Amazonians', statuesque women of the tribe. The first ascent of the river was made in 1638 by Pedro Texiera, a Portuguese, who reached Quito by the Napo river. The upper river was first used commercially when rubber was exploited in the Amazon forests. With the vast increase in the demand for rubber the price rose and Indians were press-ganged into gathering it over a wide area of the forest. Thousands of them died. There was a great public scandal. The forest Indians have not forgotten what happened and this is partly the reason why hundreds of tribes will not venture near to, let alone go across the line between barbarity and civilization, but remain in their own territory unseen by white man. Around 1910, when rubber prices were at their best, thousands of tons of rubber were exported in all kinds of river boats, many of which capsized because they were badly made. After the plantation rubber trees in the East Indies had gained maturity just before the first World War, Amazon rubber was scarcely worth collecting, especially in view of the difficulties encountered. By 1915 the only big industry in this primitive region collapsed. There was another unexpected revival of rubber collecting for a short period ending 1927, in which year the total amount exported was 29,000 long tons.

The Amazon was then divided into three trading areas. These were Belem, ninety miles from the open sea and slightly south of the Equator; Manaus, a remote town about 1,000 miles up river; and Iquitos. Like Manaus, Iquitos tried to look modern with its squares, shopping centres and hotels but both were far from the outside world. The population felt hopelessly cut off and the towns were mouldering and shabby. No roads radiated out from either place. They remained collecting centres for the produce of a vast area, some part of it unchartered and unmapped.

"I wouldn't go again up the Amazon, myself," a Peruvian traveller told me, "but you'd be a fool if *you* didn't go. Iquitos is your starting point. Go up river and live among the Indians.

They'll not kill you. Then you'll see how part of the world has stood still while the rest of it has forged ahead."

I soon discovered there was no direct route from Machu Picchu to Iquitos by air, sea or overland. Between the two places lay a vast unsurmountable barrier, the eastern slopes of the Andes, covered with sub-tropical forest up to a height of 11,000 feet, and with jungle, impenetrable and unexplored except by the Ucayali and its tributaries. These waterways travel through the dense jungle for 1,000 miles. This 'no man's land for a white man' is about 60 per cent of all Peruvian territory. It contains only 8 per cent of the total population of the country. There are, in fact, between nought and nine persons per square mile— forest Indians in small, widely scattered tribes of barbaric people estimated by the enumerators at the last census to number 1,200,000. I believe the number is far higher. Of course, these are only part of the Indian community.

My best plan, I learned, was to go by Faucett plane from Cuzco to Lima, where, so I was told, I could get another Faucett plane to Iquitos, a distance, according to the current South American Handbook, of 1,200 miles. The alternative to the air journey was cheaper but less certain. I could go by road for 300 miles to Pucallpa on the Ucayali river. This would take me a variable time according to whether rain made the road impassable, whether my vehicle stood the test and whether the road beyond San Alejandro was open. Then I could go from Pucallpa on a steamer to Iquitos, taking about five days.

I elected to go to Lima by plane and continue in the same way to Iquitos. I am a poor adventurer, especially towards the end of a journey.

I obtained a window seat in the plane from Cuzco to Lima with the intention of trying to identify inhabited places on the ground with the help of a new map of Peru just published by the *Geographical Magazine*. A Peruvian officer on leave from the Sierra occupied the next seat to mine and at once tried to air his English which he had learned from a text-book and the radio. Finally he asked me if I had noticed a Quechua-speaking teenager, a girl of Inca descent, in a seat to our left. I had not and remedied the omission. The girl was certainly worth looking at. She had the same colouring as Peta but she had the looks of a beauty queen.

"That girl's a model," said the officer at the back of his hand. "She's one of the highest paid models in South America."

" She looks it," I said.

" Well groomed?"

" More than well groomed," I said.

" Then you should have seen her a year ago."

The officer then told me a remarkable story which I have no reason to doubt. He said he was in the Sierra with a party of climbers which included a well known artist and his wife, when they had seen a girl on the outskirts of a primitive village in one of the ridges where the Incas had hidden centuries ago from the Spaniards. The girl had stared at the party, then uttered a little scream and raced away like the wind. She had been scantily dressed and was obviously terrified of strangers; she had rarely if ever, seen a white man. The artist commented on the beauty and natural elegance and grace of the girl as they ate an *al fresco* lunch and his wife agreed that she had the makings of a model. The army officer said he had never seen a girl so vividly beautiful or with so lovely a figure and he was intrigued to know where she lived. The party decided to go into the village. They found a few grass-topped huts which were mere platforms on stilts where the Indians slept nearly naked in bunks slung one on top of the other. They found the girl peering out in terror from behind a tree. The artist's wife tried to make contact with her without success for the girl merely ran away. One of the party spoke Quechua and he was able to locate the father of the girl. He told the man that the artist's wife was willing to train his daughter in Lima to be a dress model, but the man had heard neither of Lima nor of dress models. It took an hour to make the Indian understand, and then only with the help of his neighbours. The man made an animal call with his cupped hands and the girl appeared like a ghost in the clearing near the primitive hut where she lived. She was told of the offer which had been made and to the surprise of everyone she smiled happily. Although she was filthy, her clothes in rags, her hair matted and straggling down to her slim waist, she apparently had enough intelligence to realize that she was being offered a chance to leave the valley and go into the big world outside. No one in the valley, least of all the girl, had ever been to a town. They had, in fact, never wandered far from their homes because of the belief that spirits haunted a nearby mountain. It was agreed that the artist and his wife should return at a certain time and take the girl to Lima, register her, since she had never been counted in a census, buy her clothes, groom her, find her accommodation and later teach her the rudiments of the art of modelling clothes.

"I presume," I said, as the officer rambled on, "that the girl over there is the one you're talking about?"

"Believe it or not, yes. I saw her on the airfield at Cuzco and thought there was something familiar about her. I asked the woman photographer where I might have seen her before. She told me that the girl had been transformed from a little barbarian into a fashionable young lady in under a year. She's even been taught some Spanish. She has had lessons in speech, manners, deportment and been given elementary education, of the kind infants would be given. She was absolutely ignorant, was not even house trained. She mastered half a dozen clichés, such as some girls today use at every social occasion. The photographer did not tell me the worst, but I gather it was very much like bringing up a puppy, teaching it how to go about things. Now, they can't keep men away from her. All kinds of men try to date her, even one of the celebrities in Lima. They have had to refuse to let her out of sight. The girl is still under tuition. They fear they will not be able to hold her back for long. Under her warpaint she is still something of a savage, and she's getting to know her way about and is developing all the feminine guile for luring men."

I tried to examine the mountains south of Cuzco after we had become airborne but the officer had been alone at his station too long to remain silent.

"Wait," he said in my ear, "and I'll bet my month's pay she'll be in the crew compartment in the next twenty miles."

I smiled, and forgot the remark until, a little later, a member of the crew came through the curtains above, looked round quickly, and made straight for the model. He halted beside her and spoke but a few words. There was some difference of opinion but the Indian girl, her dark features wreathed in smiles, rose quickly and walked ahead of the airman. It was not long before she vanished into the crew compartment. She walked with the ease and grace of a dancer.

"What did I tell you?" asked the officer. "We'll not see her again until we get to Lima. You watch."

And we did not. The woman photographer had obviously been told not to let the girl out of her sight. She was so perturbed she called a hostess and sent a precautionary message to her charge.

Lima is said to be the architectural gem of the Pacific, but when

I had been in the city for a few days I thought it looked more attractive from the air. It is possible from a height to appreciate the beauty of its situation, between the blue sea and the chocolate-brown foothills, with the Andes rising behind them, range upon range until the horizon is etched by the perpetually snow-covered peaks of giants that rise to over 20,000 feet.

The city was founded by Pizarro on 18th January, 1535, only twenty-five months after he had overcome the Incas. He saw it as the capital of Spanish South America (which it later became) as well as capital of Peru, replacing Cuzco. He had found Cuzco too cold and too remote from the Pacific, on which he relied for his communications. Pizarro called Lima 'The City of Kings', an ambitious title when all it comprised at first were a few blocks of buildings, mainly of imported materials. He grouped these buildings into lots and handed them over to 117 of his fellow bandits, setting apart at the same time the sites of, and laying the corner-stones for, the cathedral, the Palace of the Viceroys and the Municipal Palace. The University of San Marcos, the first in America, was not founded until sixteen years later, just before the Inquisition, which lasted until 1813.

The new capital became the first home in America of successive bands of Spaniards which came over the Atlantic in search of loot in the wake of Columbus, of artisans brought from Spain to develop the colony and of rich settlers lured to 'The New Spain' by fabulous accounts of its beauty and wealth.

The city became known as Lima, a Spanish derivation of the Indian name for the river Rimac, on the banks of which it developed. Although great squares like the Plazas San Martin, De Armas, Bolivar, Union and De Mayo and wide thoroughfares like Wilson, Tacne and Nicolas de Pierola came to be built, the early city centre remains very much as it was. The streets, *jirons*, they are called, are of the same width as Pizarro thought necessary to accommodate the few horses he introduced into the country. They are today incapable of coping with modern two-way traffic and the city fathers have ingeniously saved themselves a vast new rebuilding project by adapting Pizarro's early plan to a neat traffic system. All the streets are straight and at right angles to each other so that if viewed from above that part of the city that stretches from Plaza Union to Plaza Bolivar and the avenue Nicolas de Pierola to the Rimac river is like a draughtboard, divided into over sixty squares or intersections, of more or less the same size. The council decreed that the problem of the too narrow streets could be solved by making them all one way streets so that the traffic could go up one street and down the other parallel to it. The plan works perfectly with the aid of traffic beacons and theatrical-looking traffic policemen. Visitors are able in comfort to walk in the face of oncoming one way traffic and see the old buildings in comparative safety. In this old part of the town I liked the old domestic architecture far better than the over-ornate churches which flicker with thousands of candles, glitter with hundreds of gold bejewelled images, swirl with sickening clouds of incense and whine with battalions of beggars.

The old houses were mostly in Moorish style with great sculptured balconies and Andalusian grilled windows through which, in the past, lovely *tapadas* flirted coyly with serenading suitors in the streets below. One of the finest such buildings was the palace of the Marquis de Torre Tagle, a pure seventeenth century example of the Sevillian " tawdry " style, below which, so I was assured, jealous rivals for the hand of the same beauty fought protracted duels to the death. Many of these graceful buildings, the work of romantics, have successfully resisted several earthquakes. Carved cedar ceilings, beautiful Moorish-style carved balconies and ornate doors are as perfect as on the day they were made.

There is little doubt old Lima was an unbridled expression of the vainglorious character of the Spanish people in the heyday of their colonialism as well as a prodigal demonstration in over-decorated temples to their arrogant belief that their god was the one and only true god. This was the new Spain and it set aside a tithe of its treasure, squeezed out of the real owners of the land, to embellish, as they thought, an everlasting shrine to Spanish achievement. Bermal Diaz put the whole thing into a nutshell when he said in *The True History of the Conquest of the New Spain* that the Spaniards had gone to South America " in the service of God and the King and to give light to those who were in darkness and to wax rich as all men wish to do." The Spanish were the vainest of all viceroys according to what I could see in museums and read in libraries. The Viceroy and his family were wont to ride about the streets of the City of Kings like tinpot gods in gold and scarlet carriages with footmen in elaborate livery followed by knights mounted on horses decorated with harness flashing with silver, and with velvet trappings studded

with jewels. As this theatrical entourage moved about the streets
the Viceroy would bow sedately to the adulatory crowds standing
outside the big houses with carved balconies and tiled patios, to
the reverential throngs of bearded and bedecked priests outside
the churches and to the subservient civic leaders in robes outside
the administrative offices. The wretched descendants of the Incas
if there at all, crouched in dark corners to escape punishment
from the military.

It is not easy, even while watching the comic-opera perfor-
mance of the guard outside the government house in the Plaza de
Armas, or examining the equestrian statue of Pizarro with helmet
and sword, to visualize clearly what old Lima was like, to separate
the embellishments of old from the purely utilitarian of today, the
carved wood and the sculptured stone from the glaring white
concrete skyscrapers, mountains of boxes for people that rear ugly
heads twenty storeys over the tops of gracefully beautiful houses
of early days. To look at the skyline from, for instance, the top
of the hotel Crillon, as I did, is to ask to be put off one's ordered
meal. Surely nothing is so revolting as a confusion of glass and
steel skyscrapers, at times smothered with jarring colours, alongside proportionately built houses for one family which reveal the
work of real craftsmen.

When I looked down into the streets the only upturned faces
I saw, and these covered with bewilderment, were those of the
descendants of the Incas. These pathetic survivors of empire had
been forced to walk from their remote smallholdings in the high
Sierra, still barefoot and wearing pathetically picturesque garb,
because drought had ruined their crops. They wandered about like
ghosts, too proud to beg and not knowing where to turn for help.
The most pathetic groups I saw stood in the lee of the wind near to
primitive cooking apparatus on street corners from which were
sold *anticuchos*—beef cut into cubes, broiled on skewers over an
open charcoal fire and then smothered with hot red pepper sauce.
As I watched them I thought of Philip II, a Spaniard with
humanity in his heart, who interfered with his exploiting subjects
in South America to ask if his vassals, for that was what the Incas
had become, were ill-treated and if their oppressors were
punished. I also remembered Francisco de Vitoria, the originator
of the concept of international law, who pleaded that the government of the descendants of the Incas should be entrusted to people
of intelligence and experience who would govern in the welfare

and interest of the Indians and not merely for the profit of the Spaniards. But just as the Incas had seen the Spanish pioneers fall out and fight each other over the distribution of the spoils, keeping even that which the Spanish crown wanted for its own bulging coffers, so the Incas now saw their fellow nationals competing with each other fiercely in a commerce they, as primitive agriculturalists, did not understand. Such city dwellers had little time for the Indians though they were better off than in the days when Spain set up in Peru the first European colonial service. The French historian, Raynal, prophesied that a revolution would come out of America as a result of the great gulf between the disinherited native and the wealthy invader. He thought that just as such places in America had been devastated and exploited so the New World would exploit and probably rule the Old World. He even went so far as to say that South America would be the refuge for European people who had been driven out of their homes by politics or war. The actual revolution came after Napoleon's occupation of Spain, and the abdication of Charles IV. What he did not say, and what was evident to me, and not only in the faces of these wretchedly poor refugees from the Sierra, was that all the material for a revolution in South America existed as a result of the great gulf which exists between the Indians and the creoles (American-born Spaniards). Their one aim seemed to be to feather their own nests, to set up beautiful homes in such luxury quarters as San Isidro and Miraflores, to mention but two. These garden cities contrasted sadly with the terrible slums about which the visiting Director of Public Cleanliness of Westminster, Mr. F. McCarthy, made a critical report.

The sight of the bewildered creatures made me all the keener to get to Iquitos and from there up the Amazon, where the outcasts of Peruvian society live across the frontier separating civilization from savagery. I decided to go at once to a travel office to see when I could start the journey.

E*

XVIII

Living Art

UNKNOWN TO me, the man with whom I was to travel up the Amazon from Iquitos, Richard L. Brown, art editor of the *Kansas City Star*, which belongs to one of the biggest newspaper organizations in the United States, landed at Trujillo, on the coast to the north at about the same time I arrived in Lima.

Both of us apparently had the same idea, first to take a look at the coast, then go to Iquitos. It was much more likely that we should have met first on the coast, instead of, as it transpired, in our hotel at the side of the fever-infested Amazon. However, the coast is a vast place, a mainly desert strip, 1,400 miles long and between fifty and a hundred miles wide.

I forgot to ask Brown later what made him turn his attention to the desert when his major interest lay in the Amazon. Probably it was because there was so much to see to occupy a man with his wide interests. He might even have been delayed there in his flight to Iquitos, as I was in Lima, and merely filled in time; but I hardly believe that. As he wrote later in the *Kansas City Star*, " All I meant to do was test the desert dust with the toe of my shoe, but I uncovered a fragment of pottery.

" The clay," he said, " might have been shaped by Inca hands, or by some artist craftsman of some earlier and even more skilful civilization." The shard reminded him that man's art is his most permanent achievement.

My own interest in the coast was aroused when I visited two museums in Lima. They were the National Museum of Art, which contains nearly 7,000 exhibits, giving a chronological history of Peruvian cultures and art from the 2,500 year old Paracas civilization, to the present time, and the Museum of Anthropology and Archaeology, which has remarkable relics of the aboriginal races of Peru, textiles from Paracas and ceramics of Chimu, Nazca, Pachacamac and the Inca cultures. What impressed me most was the uniquely obscene pottery of the Mochica period (A.D. 400-800).

Like Brown, I found pottery of the old pre-Inca and Inca cultures was more impressive than the metal work, the weaving or the architecture, although these taught us fascinating facts about nearly thirty distinct Peruvian cultures which flourished in a period of 3,000 years. During all that time not a single word was written about any one of them. Two scribes from either side of the Atlantic tried, therefore, in their modest ways to pick up a clue here and a clue there to piece together a picture as if on some great jigsaw puzzle. In so doing we were to learn as much as we could have done, and in a quicker, far more vivid and pleasurable way, as if we had read a complete history of the period. In one way I was pleased there was no written history; that these great cultures had no written language. I was able to exercise my imagination to the full, to draw my own conclusions from inanimate objects instead of having everything spelled out for me.

Along the whole route of the coast from Tumbes to Tacna we probably found between us that there are twenty widely separated areas which are irrigable, most of them alongside such rivers as the Tumbes, Mache, Viru, Santa and Rimac. There are in all fifty ' rivers ' but in actual fact only ten of them carry water all the year round. The other forty are either seasonally dry or mere wadis. Over a million acres of desert at the irrigable points have been cultivated to provide forty fat green fingers of oases which reach out into the dun-coloured sand. In the north, at one of the irrigable parts, Quiroz, Peru's most profitable crop, cotton, is grown, and this provides 20 per cent of the country's exports. Below Lima sugar and rice flourish on the oasis. In the south, grapes and melons and olives are the main crops.

The 1,400-mile-long coast of Peru is scorched by the blazing sun all the year round. The upper part of the coast, between 2,500 and 6,500 feet high, is barren and repelling with its arid denial of life. The lower part is less repugnant only in so far as cacti grow among the outcrops of rock. North of Lima is the acme of sterility, the Sechura desert, as inhospitable in parts as the Western Desert of Africa in which I became native with the desert rat. In prehistoric times this long Peruvian coast was the cradle of strange and mysterious empires whose relics, ruined temples, crazy ceramics, beautiful textiles and gold and silver ornaments, are the pride and joy of some of the world's best museums. Even to this day I found grave robbers despoiling tombs that have remained intact for long centuries, bringing up treasures that had been placed by loved ones within the reach of the person there buried.

It seemed to me that but for two practices, that of burying the dead in mummy bundles in the dry sand of the rainless coast and of designing remarkably detailed portrait pottery modelled in clay, the world would know few personal facts about the Inca and pre-Inca cultures. Between them, the mummies and the vases tell posterity far more about the Incas and some of their predecessors than all the ruins that have survived. They told us what the people wore, what they ate and how they lived, and loved, as well as how abominably they sinned and how they suffered.

Mummies wrapped in striking Inca tapestries were found squatting on their haunches, knees drawn up to their head, their hands clasped on their knees. Besides the bodies of the men were the objects they had used in their lifetime in war, at work and at play. There were primitive weapons, tools and sporting equipment, generally fishing tackle or weapons used when hunting wild animals in the Andes. There were always collections of coca leaves which proved how universal was the habit of chewing the cocaine-producing plant. There were always superstitious charms to ward off evil spirits or propitiate the many gods.

The mummy of a woman was generally surrounded with objects of domestic use. These were spindles, pottery in which to hold spices in the kitchen or baskets woven out of reeds which contained threads used in the making of tapestry or clothes. The mummified remains, in an excellent state of preservation, showed the Incas to be thickset and of medium height, with big heads and faces with pronounced features, great aquiline noses with huge nostrils, heavily lidded, rather protruding eyes, high cheek bones and pronounced jaws which gave them a look of great granite determination and phenomenal strength. The women were generally not beautiful in face or in figure though an occasional mummy, delicately encased in finely woven tapestry, displayed aristocratic good looks. The men wore the *huara,* or breechcloth, a type of bush jacket called the *uncu,* a thick warm poncho which resembled a sack with a slit through which to put the head, sometimes fitted with a cowl-like hood. The women wore flounced petticoats one above the other, all of them edged with gaily decorated tapestry, bright shawls and a wide-brimmed flat hat capable of being decorated. Over their day clothes the women wore at night the *luclla*, or mantle, kept in place by a silver pin. Both men and women wore belts, sandals and ornaments on the fingers, in the ears and on their wrists. Remains of meals proved that they ate llama meat, guinea pigs, deer, potatoes, tomatoes, maize and beans. The favourite drink was *chicha*, a potent beverage made from corn, and is universally popular today. The Incas regarded Viracocha, the Creator, as their supreme god, but they were hedged in by numerous spirits, good and bad, which manifested themselves in a variety of ways.

The pottery made by the Incas was durable, artistic, domestically useful. I have seen vessels in the shape of peasants' houses revealing to scale shape and size and such characteristics as thatched roofs; vessels of vegetables, or a bunch of vegetables; of male and female peasants; of nobles, priests and even of surgeons operating, setting broken bones or amputating limbs. All of the pottery is artistically decorated and has on it traditional figures of the Incas, heads of llamas, pumas, jaguars and various kinds of colourful birds. More interesting than the pure Inca pottery was that left behind by the Mochica and the Chimus, the last pre-Inca people, whom the Incas defeated. The Incas may have learned the art of pottery making from these people.

The first pottery made in Peru, some 3,000 years ago, was plain and utilitarian and has little to commend it. At the other end of the scale pottery made by the Mochica-Chimu civilization (A.D. 400–1,000) before the Incas conquered them is unique in the world. The Mochicas buried their pottery in the graves with the dead and in so doing not only gave perfect portraits for posterity of the deceased people, but also depicted in a vivid, often disgusting way, their vices and their sexual aberrations, as well as their lawful pursuits and pastimes. It was stated in 1964 that some 40,000 pieces of Mochica-style pottery are to be found in one Lima collection.

I was taken to many graves along the coast, some still intact and guarded, but most of them already pilfered, which told more of the Mochica than books would have done. They contained or had contained, gold ornaments, feather ornaments, cloth and an infinite variety of pottery, ceramic-like caricatures and portraitures, which has been called the language of the Mochica. Each piece is full of minute detail eloquent of the dress, habits, diseases, sins, sports and achievements of the people. The Mochica and the Chimus provide evidence of, with a notable interval, a continuous archaeological history from the fourth century to 1461. It is remarkable that two such cultures could have continued for so many centuries in the same arid region. The desert preserved complete evidence of the culture as it preserved even in the minutest detail the corpses, their clothes, jewels and other possessions. The pottery made specially to put in the graves was intentionally designed to 'immortalize' the people there buried. Doctors have compared vivid details revealing specific diseases in both the corpse and the portrait in pottery. Shown with great faithfulness are such features as squints, spinal curvatures, bow legs, hooked noses, pierced ears, receding or protruding chins and wry necks, moles, scars and pockmarks.

Dr. Abner Weisman, a clinical professor of obstetrics and gynaecology in America, is of the opinion that the ceramics could even be a guide to the pathology of the past. Certain of the Peruvain figurines were in fact obviously meant to tell a medical story. One figure, a well-preserved Peruvian drinking-vessel, had a black spotted face, and black hands and lips which were partly eaten away. These were clear symptoms of leprosy. Others showed ravages of smallpox, cancer, dropsy, malnutrition, and gave evidence of amputation and other surgery executed a thousand years before Columbus. Pregnancy, an annual event in the lives of most young women of the time, was clearly shown. Of one girl, depicted in pottery, he said, " She was only eleven or twelve and I think she was worried about the baby."

A series of works showing midline incisions suggested that Caesarean sections may have been common. Facial features were minutely drawn to reveal the lines caused by worry, or age, or suffering. It was at times almost possible to guess the character of a person depicted by expressions suggestive of refinement, greed, cruelty, avarice and especially, since many of the ceramics related to men and women in the act of fornication, the unbridled lust and passion and vitality awakened by each in the other. The artists seemed always to aim at stark realism concealing nothing, revealing everything. There was no evidence of clients being flattered by romantic portrayals or polite untruths. The people portrayed paid in kind and the portraits were carefully executed in

fine material and coloured realistically. One could only conclude
that truth, not flattery, was what was sought.

Some of the effigy pottery showing the Mochica engaged in acts
of outrageously bestial and sensuous indulgence is not fit to be
seen by anyone. Men are shown vividly in the act of sodomizing
men or women, or of having intercourse with women in a variety
of ways, sometimes openly, sometimes secretly at night as others
slept nearby. There are innumerable elaborate pieces of pottery
tableaux showing close-up views of men and women being intimate even as the women are engaged in domestic tasks. There are
many highly offensive tableaux depicting fellatio, which appears
to have been a frequent preliminary to sexual intercourse. The
figures are remarkably lifelike, even if the male sexual organ is
grossly enlarged. Facial expressions reveal vividly the lust and
passion of the participants. One much-prized coloured vase
depicts an enthroned nobleman enjoying almost ceremoniously
the act of fellatio performed by a young girl. Even the foulest
ceramics are so lifelike that the potter (such work was performed
by women) must have modelled their designs on scenes in real
life maybe witnessed by stealth unknown to the ' models '. There
are also vases depicting animals, bats, cats, owls, foxes, jaguars,
bears, snakes, deers, monkeys, some of them also in the act of
intercourse. The Mochicas were obviously obsessed with sex in its
most hideous guises.

What is surprising is that the characters depicted so realistically in the most intimate actions of their lives apparently did not
object. They did not smash the pottery and assault the artists.
Stirrup cups containing incriminating evidence of the sins of the
deceased were indeed given places of honour by the relatives who,
for some reason no one can determine, were very proud to per-
petuate evidence of such pastimes. The Incas found the Mochica-
Chimu, when they defeated them in 1460-1470, to be so addicted
to sexual vices that leaders pleaded with them to return to normal
copulation and so procreate their kind. The Spanish did the same
in the seventeenth century. One Spanish priest said that the
people " are very inclined to sodomy and even up to this day
(1638) they are not free of this contagious sexual habit. Once they
did it with men, now they do it with women and hide their vice
under the cover of matrimony, thus preventing human generation
by this form of sexuality." Another wrote about the slight importance the Indians attached to the virginity of their wives so long

as they were willing to partake in the abominable sin of sodomy. The writer had heard that before the bride was deflowered in marriage the husband sated his illicit lusts upon her. In spite of the fact that there was an abundance of women, many of them good looking, most men were given to the vice. The pottery shows clearly that the women, as well as the men, took great pleasure in the vice which may have originated in religion. Youths were attached to the temples so that nobles and chieftains who attended official feasts in them could afterwards satisfy their abominable lust. There is no doubt that the pottery which commemorates this fact is unique as pornography; but it has been preserved mainly because it gives the only clear record of the lives of the Mochica-Chimu people.

It was not long after Richard Brown and I had begun separately to travel along the coast that it became apparent to me that the greatest craftsmen and artists lived along the arid desert coast. There were many Mochica and Chimu sites in the north, among them the crumbling adobe ruins of Chan-Chan, imperial city of the Chimu Empire, which stretched over a score of valleys between the Gulf of Guayaquil and Southern Peru. This was overcome by the Incas but they did not destroy the place. The Spaniards, who came later, despoiled the burial mounds of all the gold and silver statuettes and ornaments and jewels buried with the Chimu nobles. The city walls, which enclose an area of nearly ten square miles, had inside them the ruins of palaces, temples and domestic premises, all of them showing signs of artistic decorations and painted patterns. At the southern limit of the Chimu Empire (A.D. 1000–1466) is the comparatively small area where the Chavin Culture thrived from 1200 to 400 B.C. Even experts, who have devoted years to its study, are baffled by a unique mysterious civilization with a perfect art form, based four square on the strangest mythology known to man. A precautionary government has, of course, removed many of the treasures, among them the obelisk found in the main plaza of the Fortress of Chavin, the Raimondi stele, tracings of the friezes from the temple, and a remarkable collection of ' speaking pottery '.

Much of the sculpture found in the museums and on the sites reveal fantastic and diabolical creatures born in the fevered imaginations of the artists as well as real people and idealized beings. In the main the artists were inspired to produce five mythological creatures in the Chavin culture, the most horrible of which is an hermaphroditic dragon with a large-fanged muzzle, clawed feet and a cavernous mouth and teeth in its stomach There are also anthropomorphic feline monsters with a crown of feline heads and sceptres, or arms, in both hands, a humanized ornithomorphic monster, part bird, part serpent with feline heads, a heavily scaled icthomorphic monster and a feline with cadavarous human features. Five monsters are to be found on pieces of sculpture, pottery, stones and ornaments. The Chavin pottery is more astonishing than the ornaments. It is of one colour, black or reddish brown, with sculptured ornamentation of real or mythological beings. Characteristic of the pottery is a round shape with cylindrical neck and curved tubular handles.

One man, Miguel Mujica Gallo, of Lima, who for nearly twenty years has been collecting pre-Spanish gold, has a remarkable collection of gold objects made by the Chimu. He began to collect the treasures when he was offered two gold knives of the Chimus culture by an old man. The man revealed that he had a collection of them and that he would sell them all or none at all. He had already received a tempting offer for them from an American museum. Miguel Mujica Gallo could not resist the temptation and bought the collection which is now safely preserved for posterity in a subterranean museum. Pieces show that the Chimu were most expert in the delicate art of working in gold. Among many fine exhibits are gold Chimu lances, a gold wailing mask (made all in one piece) whose tears are two emeralds; a ceremonial poncho comprised of 13,000 gold pieces; gold Chimu helmets made of long plates fashioned after banana leaves; masks with Colombian emeralds; warriors' necklaces adorned with Caribbean pearls and ear ornaments like that I recovered for Peta. Although all the exhibits are fabulously beautiful the finest of them all is a great urn which has two golden arms and hands with silver nails which glitter under the lights of the gallery.

On the coast a few miles below is Paramonga, once the final boundary of the 600-mile long kingdom of the Chimu. Here is the site of the most important *huacas* (shrine) on the coast, the fortress on the estuary of Rio Fortaleza which was the key point of a vast network of fortifications against the Incas in the south.

Below, in the Lurin valley, are the remains of the shrine of Pachacamac, the centre of a cult which greatly influenced the Chimu and which was named after the creator-hero of the moon and husband of Mama Cocha, goddess of the sea. It was of the gold treasures of Pachacamac that Pizarro heard while on his triumphant way to Cuzco but it was his equally unscrupulous brother who looted it and destroyed many of its buildings. The aqueduct system which brings water down under the ground for over twenty miles from the Andean foothills is still used by two farmers whose land is situated near the adobe ruins. The primitive dwellers here built a pyramid, in homage to an invisible and omnipotent god although they could have heard nothing about the pyramids of Egypt and elsewhere. The Incas were so impressed by it that they respected it when they conquered the area and, in fact, built in the same place a greater temple-pyramid dedicated to sun worship. They also built other temples to the goddesses Moon and Urpy Wachac, all of them decorated with an abundance of pure gold and a large number of jewels.

Still lower down there was Paracas, where the earliest archaeological evidences of Peruvian cultures on the coast were found, as well as magnificently embroidered mantles, in which the mummies of some 400 nobles of Paracas had sat in their graves for over a millenium. No one can say with certainty who were these talented people, or how long ago they lived. Such mantles as these, examples of which are to be found in Lima's museums, did not impress Brown so much as the textiles of Inca-Nazca culture (A.D. 400–1438) which blossomed a few miles to the south.

"At the disposal of the Nazcas," wrote Brown later, "were nearly all the major weaving techniques and materials except that for silk. They did not have flax, but did use other types of plant fibre. The finest materials, though, were the llama, alpaca and vicuna. It appears that most Nazca textiles were prepared for burial purposes, and from graves along the southern coast have come some almost unbelievable examples. They employ twining, repp, twill, brocade, tapestry, embroidery, gauze, lace, knitting, painted and resist-dye decoration, and many other techniques. Some experts have said that it would be impossible with modern machinery to reproduce such fineness. It is not rare, in Nazca textiles to find up to three hundred wool threads to the inch. One of the amazing aspects of this virtuosity in weaving is that not just a few, but many, many examples remain of the same high quality, suggesting that there were large numbers of skilled weavers. As many as two hundred hues in seven colour ranges occur in complex, repeated patterns, both pictorial and geometric.

It is easy to say that the Peruvians had the great advantage of the long, soft wool of the alpacas and vicunas—but the difficulty of planning and weaving a patterned textile on a simple back-strap loom is incredible. The weavers had to visualize the design before starting, then calculate and memorize the steps toward producing it—all without writing or any visual aid to memory."

The name Nazca, a fabulous area still lower down the coast is redolent of mystery. It fills my mind with strange speculations founded on a conversation between two Anglo-Peruvians I over-heard on a long train journey. The word Nazca kept cropping up in the conversation and they connected it with a mystery. Some people, they said, thought that the inhabitants of another planet had descended centuries ago in flying saucers guided to Nazco by straight lines drawn on the arid landscape nearby. These mysterious lines and figures were on the stone-covered pampa at Ingenio. They could do nothing but guide skymen, or men from another world, to land. In addition to the lines there were wonderful pictures, so big that they must have been drawn, to have perspective and continuity and the right proportions, by someone guiding the artist from high above. The drawings are unique: there is nothing remotely like them anywhere.

It was not long after that conversation in the train that I found Nazca near the coast. The town of the same name was colonial, of Spanish origin, with about 20,000 population, lying in a pleasant green valley surrounded by forbidding mountains some 2,000 feet above the Pacific. The Nazcas, after whom the town is named, were a highly developed people whose culture reached its maximum about A.D. 800. As one can see in the local museum and in many museums in the Old World, the Nazcas made beautifully decorated ceramics, fine wood carvings and gold objects of great delicacy. They lived in the valley and worshipped at the Temple of the Sun. They were not only great artists but engineers. The reservoir of Bisambra nearby enabled the Nazcas to pipe water through underground aqueducts to water the land. At least half a dozen are still to be seen and one or two are in use after over a thousand years.

Eagerly, I asked about the Nazca lines (which can be seen and fully appreciated only from an aeroplane) only to find that they are as much a puzzle to the natives as they were to me. " You must find Dr. Marie Reiche," I was told time and again. " She is a great mathematician and she has spent much of her life in the desert trying to find the answer to the puzzle. Even she cannot be sure what they mean."

The lines had been seen, but not in their entirety, by Peruvian Indians many years ago. It was not until the coming of the aeroplane, however, that the lines were seen as a whole, and their implication realized. They were reported to the archaeological authorities by the first airman to see them. Experts flew in small planes over the desert taking pictures of them, making drawings and examining them from every possible angle. At times the lines looked like a ground map of some elaborate railway network with junctions, excepting that they covered hundreds of square miles around the valley and that they had been there long before railways were invented. What puzzled mathematicians most was that the lines were perfectly straight over a vast area of varying elevation, as if drawn with supernatural guidance. Sometimes they seemed to describe motor race tracks, or runways—miles long and perfectly straight—on which to land from the air. Here and there between obviously intentional breaks in the lines are monstrously large drawings of animals and birds as if they were part of a myserious code used in signalling to the sky. The creatures were accurately drawn as if the artist had been able to keep in view throughout his draughtsmanship not just a tiny proportion of the whole which would have fallen into the orbit of a normal man, but the whole figure, even if the landscape varied in altitude. One of the theories held by Maria Reiche was that the straight lines mark the rising and setting points of the moon and some of the planets and stars, but if this is so the significance of the pictures of animals and birds are still a puzzle. People disagree as to when the lines were drawn. Some say they have been on the valley crust for not longer than a thousand years while others, Maria Reiche among them, think that they were executed many centuries before that. Flying over the desert one can make out the outline of a great condor in flight, a tremendous leviathan, and a creepy-crawly object with long bent legs. They are like creatures out of some nightmare or they have their origin in another world. The New World, so called, studied heavenly bodies, the sun, moon, planets and stars, long before we did. If Maria Reiche is right the heavens were studied long before the Children of the Sun came into their own—by what people we do not know.

It was at Nazcas and Paracas that I saw burial grounds, now

empty, and some of their contents, now jealously preserved. Between the two world wars American-Peruvian excavators discovered in the burial grounds some beautiful textiles which cannot be improved on. They were in an excellent state of preservation the bright colours full of contrast and lustre. The foreman on a nearby sugar plantation showed me a collection of highly painted stones obviously stolen by grave robbers and sold when in need of cash. He said that one could often buy little objects a thousand years old from workers on the cotton fields or the orange fields. Nazca and its desert area was the home of some of the greatest pre-Inca civilizations which centred on Temples of the Sun, the chief of which (at Trujillo) is said to have contained about 1,500,000 adobe bricks. These early people might have been apprentices to the mummy makers of Egypt. They efficiently deviscerated their dead, then dried the corpses in the sun and finally buried them in graves of sand which would preserve them.

The idea of mummifying the corpses was based in the belief that the dead were transported by magic to another land. For this reason they were not bound up in mummy cloths, which would restrict movement, but loosely wrapped in textiles made specially for the purpose.

XIX

The Chincha Islands

ON MY way back to Lima, thence to fly to Iquitos, I made a tour
by motor boat of offshore islands, including the Chincha Islands,
innocent of the fact that in doing so I had chosen one of the most
important centenary anniversaries of the Republic for the purpose.
It was a hundred years to the very day when the Spanish who
had ruled Peru from the sixteenth century until the revolutionary
war of 1821-4, also visited the very same islands, but with a quite
different purpose. I made the tour for my amusement because
I had grown tired of ancient civilizations and wanted to get back
into modern times. The Spaniards went to the Chincha Islands to
use them as a safe base from which to make their last futile
attempt to re-conquer the Spanish-American Empire. They had
chosen first to attack Peru, the most important of the Spanish
vice-royalties in South America, probably because it was the
scene of their first victory over the Incas. The country had declared
its independence on 28th July, 1821, though it was not until three
years later, after a long and fierce war, that Peru could actually be
said to be free.

Incidentally, the Chincha Islands, three in number, lying fourteen miles off Nazca, in the Inca Department, had also been visited
a hundred years back by another Englishman, who had been
sent out to Peru to assess the chances of exploitation of deposits
of millions of wild sea fowl (known as guano) on the offshore
islands in a planned expansion of the Peruvian economy. British
capital had been promised the year before to President Castilla
who had drawn up a scheme to try to make the country prosperous, " Bird muck " was one of the most intriguing items on the
list. The deposits—the end product of millions of sea fowl—were
found to be highly valuable, literally worth their weight in gold

even in a country where gold is mined. In one period of forty years
the Peruvian Government obtained £300,000,000 by the sale of
20,000,000 tons of bird droppings, all collected from these islands.
The first island I saw was so covered by pelicans, gannets and
cormorants that it looked like one gargantuan bird, a mass of
feathers from shore to shore. The birds were breeding and per-
forming their morning toilet. The surface of the island, and the
roofs of various buildings was covered, sometimes to a great depth,
by the very kind of white-grey substance which causes such dis-
may in British town halls or at English seaside resorts.

Even as we approached from the leeward side a strong smell
of ammonia assailed the nostrils. It is unpleasant to all but a Peruvian; to him it is like eau-de-Cologne, heady and intoxicating.
The worse the smell, the more the birds will have produced,
the less will be income tax.

I tried to satisfy my curiosity and see Gaimard's cormorants
with their long necks and bills which end in a sharp hook and the
variegated booby or the larger blue-footed gannet or the red-billed
tropic bird but I did not find this easy. The boatman completely
misunderstood my mission. He thought I was interested not in the
handsome heads of these fowl but in the back end like everyone
else in Peru. I was reminded of a horticultural squire of my
acquaintance who judged the decorated exhibits on May Day at
so many horse shows. I thought he was a lover of horses. Then
I discovered he had begun to grow mushrooms. He attended the
shows only because he got all the manure.

The idea to make a business out of collecting bird droppings, at
first a subject of ridicule, began in Peru at a most critical stage
of the national economy. A succession of civil wars between white
and meztino (half caste) generals had emptied the national coffers.
Production had dropped. Even the country's livestock was
depleted. Tax collectors did not know where to turn for the money
needed to run the country. It was then discovered that a certain
gardener was winning all the prizes with his melons, twice as
large, and early, as any others. No artificial chemical fertilizer
could have done the trick. Civic detectives got to work. They discovered that the man collected the bird droppings from Don
Martin island not far from Lima and fed it to his crop with
magical results. Experts collected some of the malodorous material
and analysed it to discover that they were penetrating an old Inca
secret. It was the best of all natural organic fertilizers used by the

Incas on the terraces. It contained deposits of nitrogen, potassium and phosphorus, essential elements in fertilizer, to such a degree that they were amazed. It was not long before the billions of sea fowl which bred on the many islands off the Pacific coast were elevated to the status of civil servants in some thirty factories (islands) which produced a valuable asset to put the exchequer right. Soon Peru was out of the red, as it still is out of the red. It has now free central bank gold and dollar reserves of 50,000,000 dollars with a solid backing for its currency of over 41 per cent in net gold and dollars; its balance of payments surplus is seven times higher than last year.

The guano industry, as it is euphonistically termed, is vast. Thousands of workers are employed gathering the end product, shipping, boxing it and despatching it to countries all over the world. People are clamouring for it but Peru is clever enough to fertilize her own crops before other people's. A fleet of boats which I saw on my cruise are named either after the productive birds, pelicans, stormy petrels, terns and gannets, or after islands where they breed. Mancora, Chinca, San Lorenzo or Don Martin. There are also laboratories, observatories and testing stations. The latest addition are several bird towns—a feathered conurbation—instead of the islands where the birds have hitherto insisted on breeding because they are safe from reptiles. The bird towns are on the sea shore. They are walled off, guarded against rats, foxes and wild cats. There are even toilet attendants on hand.

The guano industry is a boon. Yet there is one snag. As the detectives discovered, the end product is such marvellous fertilizer only because the birds feed on anchovies, billions of which move in vast schools all along the coast. The coast is washed by the cool Humboldt stream. This current brings with it tons of plankton and tiny plants, a delicacy for the anchovies. It causes great climatic changes, brings fortune and brings now and then disaster. The vast current of many billions of gallons of water which is ice cold has come from the south from time immemorial. The Incas thought it came from some demon stronghold. Recently it was thought, to come from the Antarctic. Of late it has been proved to well up from some " bottomless trough in the sea alongside the coast." Some marine experts have written in the past that sea monsters as well as huge octopuses and strange sea mammals live in these abysmal depths. When this water, moved by some inexplicable subterranean force, surfaces on the water of what is after all a tropical region, the hot winds condense and shed moisture in the sea to the despair of people in the coast who are without water for years. But clouds rise to cover the sun filtering the heat of its rays as it shines through fogs or mists that last for months. From June to December there are often heavy fogs over Lima. To the extreme south nothing grows because there is no rain. No rain has ever fallen for instance, in the Atacama desert. Normally the sea teems with anchovies and plankton on which the sea fowl feed before depositing their droppings on the islands.

On occasions, at intervals of from five to seven years, a warm current, known as El Nino, the Child, because it so often manifests itself at Christmas, flows south over the cold current and reverses the trend. Rain falls then on the northern coast, sometimes gently but often torrentially, flooding dry valleys, turning streets in towns which have no drainage into cataracts, washing away slightly built dwellings. Disaster stalks the land. The birds die in thousands if they cannot get away. The fishermen have no work. There is unemployment. Income tax goes up.

The smell eventually drove me away from the islands. Soon I was on my way to the Lima-Callao airport there to get Faucett's plane early next morning to Iquitos and the Amazon. Though I did not know it at the time Richard Brown was already there, ill in bed with a fever, in the hotel where I also was to stay.

XX

Towards Another World

I FELT I was going back to the world as it was in the Beginning. To Genesis. To the Seventh day, when He rested. I felt as if I was going to the edge of the civilized world, then, if all went well, going over the edge, to a world of darkness and savagery. There was a line between civilization and barbarity, not so arbitrary a line as that of the Equator though in this case the line is only three degrees from the Equator. Beyond the line all the riches of the earth were unexplored as were the great rain forests above it; all the virginal beauty unspoiled, nothing built on it, bored into it or even sown upon it; all the aboriginal perils untamed. I was, in short, going up the Amazon far beyond the last sizeable civilized outpost into an area which had a few months before seen raids by wild Indians on white explorers and prospectors. I was to travel into creeks and backwaters infested by alligators and boa-constrictors and many creatures unfriendly to man. Here the Indians hunt for their food by the blow pipe and are entirely primitive. I was not exaggerating when I said I would see this earth as the first man saw it.

I began to get excited about my forthcoming visit despite that I was in Lima still more than a thousand miles from the starting point, a town in the centre of the jungle where I should have to make the first decisive steps into the unknown. It would mean discomfort, heat, humidity, if nothing else, but the appeal of the Amazon lured me on, as it has lured on many men in the past. Some of them did not merely cross the line into barbarity but penetrated deep into the wilderness, into the unknown, and never returned, adding to the mystery of the jungle. The roll call of men lost in Amazonia is long and bewildering. I had no intention of adding to its number.

The edge of the beyond to me was Iquitos, the Peruvian jungle town over the Andes, where the only access and egress, except 2,200 miles along the Amazon, was by plane. The emblem of mechanical progress that had so outstripped the progress of *homo sapiens*, especially in parts of Northern Peru. Progress or no, if one came down in the jungle—and a biplane of the Peruvian air force was lost with eight men in these parts the very day before I set off—there would be little hope of rescue from the swampy, fever-infested wilderness.

I arranged to travel by a plane of the famous Faucett. Until recently, when Elmer Faucett pioneered this flight over the Andes, the 1,000 miles took two weeks by mule and canoe. A fellow passenger told me that last time he came, in 1960, he took over two weeks on the journey by what he called Old Piche's trail, and that he picked up a fever he has never quite shaken off. When Faucett made the first flight it took him from October 5th to December 27th. His machine force-landed on a sandbank on the Amazon, its propeller broken.

Once the Faucett plane had become airborne the whole adventure seemed inevitable. Sami Muadi in the pilot's seat said he wished he were coming with me up the Amazon for he had made up his mind to do this when but a boy. We reached the greatest barrier to man in South America, the mighty Andes, and began to cross them. Barren and brown at first, they had but a few settlements clinging to the mountainsides, settlements that got smaller and fewer until there were only sentinel huts over which the great condor flew. Then we reached the line of perpetual snow, an arbitrary line unlike that between civilization and savagery. Here there was nothing, as at the Beginning: vast stretches of deep, white snow, pure and undisturbed, then thick, unyielding ice and all around a vast and silent desolation as at the beginning of the world. Winds born in the mysterious powerhouse of nature whipped up the talcum of snow into snow devils a thousand feet high. The Andes receded. The plane descended to a more comfortable altitude. We were over an ocean of greenery, the jungle of Amazonia, and I stared down at it and realized that you could drop a division of troops into that great green morass and be sure that they would never be seen again. For hours I looked down on to the tops of millions of trees—one fifth of all the trees in the world are in Amazonia—seeing first the chocolate yellow tributaries of the Amazon empty of all craft, the shores deserted, then, at last, the great giant, the largest river in the world, weaving its way through fevered swamps. My aching eyes reached in vain for any sight of man, for a hut or a raft or a clearing in the trees but all was wilderness.

At times the great ' sea ' river, sometimes six miles wide, had on it great islands, loops and knots and bows, creeks and backwaters. The sun, shining from directly above me, cast the great shadow of the plane on the jungle, to reflect itself unexpectedly, like a round shattered mirror, in the watery swamplands beneath the undergrowth. It was only then I realized how impossible it would be to cross this part, why it was that the blueprints of penetration roads to link the capital up with this lost province had lain dusty in pigeonholes for years untouched. Never before have I felt how insignificant and helpless was man compared with the power of nature.

Sami warned me to look out. Iquitos would soon come into view, he said. Sitting in the crew compartment I shaded my eyes against the blinding sun and saw the outlines of this mouldering town, islanded completely by the impenetrable jungle. At first I thought it was a mirage. It did not look real, as some oases in the Western Desert did not look real when first seen. One wondered how anyone with a chance to live in a coastal town would stay for more than a day. But it was a town all right—Iquitos, its front the Amazon here, three miles or more wide, its back and sides tributaries Itaya and Nanay. The area, said Sami, was sixteen miles long by three miles wide, won by man from the jungle.

As the plane circled to land I saw hundreds of primitive grass and straw-thatched huts and floating houses crowded on the banks, in the native quarter round the sides of and on, the Amazon. It looked like a Central African native town. Within the town itself I saw cars and primitive buses going round and round on earth roads as on a fairground roundabout with no hope of ever going off the track.

Iquitos airport, a tin-roofed affair, was crowded with a Somerset Maugham crowd, officers in dress caps and drill, Indian women in white, missionaries in flowing white robes, indeed all the flotsam and jetsam of this hemmed-in town come to see new arrivals and old departures. Every flight day came the same crowd, reassuring itself it could get away, if only the army, the government or the church allowed it. Iquitos was not a popular station. It was used largely as a safe place of polite exile or banishment for misfits or tiresome people.

The heat of the sun penetrated my clothes in an instant as I left the plane, and soon, like the other passengers, I showed patches of sweat on my back. Quickly I was driven off in a jeep, its seat hot enough to fry an egg on, to the government hotel that looks right down into the Amazon, there to contemplate my next move.

The town was mouldering and the native quarter, Belen, was hideously poor and primitive, peopled by sickly looking Indians who seemed under-nourished or suffering from some wasting disease. They lived in shacks, some of which were raised over the discoloured water on stilts and some lived on the banks with the water lapping at the very entrances. Rats foraged about for offal, and great black vultures, the most sinister-looking birds of prey, hovered overhead or danced on the banks of the river as if they expected a corpse to be thrown out to them. Now and then a little dilapidated boat with an outboard motor crowded with old Indian women with wizened faces threaded its way through a floating market. There were flat punts laden with vegetables, from which old, unshaven peasants sold their produce. Water buses, wide home-made boats covered with thickly thatched roofs to keep off the sun plied for hire. Tiny children played in the water and drank of it though it contained sewage. In front of some shacks women, wearing only loin cloths, washed their underclothing, probably the only set they had. Where the river bank was high the shacks climbed one above the other and the people swarmed about them like so many ants, all of them unwashed and ill clad and with misery written on their faces.

XXI

The Mighty River

I TOLD the driver of the jeep as he took me from the airfield through the shabby jungle town to the government hotel that it was my intention, if I could find anyone to accompany me, to go up the Amazon and stay for a few days in the jungle. He said I should take care to find someone who knew the jungle. He told me that one or two people had come to Iquitos and not been seen again. The last person to vanish was a pretty Peruvian girl. She arrived by air and was never again heard of. As a result of this great care was taken to note all details of people who arrived, including where they stayed, and to make sure they left Iquitos when they checked out of the hotel.

Every word spoken by a newcomer in this remote outpost is news to someone. That was why, after I had taken a shower, a *mulatto* came to my room to say I was wanted in the lobby. I was glad to know this. Iquitos was boring in the extreme. The main occupation, apart from visiting a few poor dance halls or night clubs, was to sit on park benches in the main square where a large fountain played among the tropical trees to cool the air. People looked bored as inmates look bored. If one talked to young people the first thing they said was that they wanted to go to the United States. The promenade along the front of the Amazon was not even paved and the slightest rain churned up the road until it was like a quagmire. This did not prevent courting couples seeking the shade of the palms. The hotel offered few amenities though its vast rooms included a dense tropical indoor garden in which macaws and parrots captured in the jungle squawked and screamed at each other throughout the day and night. The only distinctive feature I can recall were the large wall paintings of romantic figures in the style of a modern Peruvian school.

I found Richard Brown of the *Kansas City Star* waiting for me. He was tall, slim and mouse-quiet. I thought he was the most sweet-natured man I had met until he told me what he thought of the food, much of it inedible, and the wall paintings. He is an expert on art and on food and must suffer a good deal in his quest for typical national dishes.

After we had introduced ourselves to each other, and explained why we had come, we found we had both spent some time on Peru's desert coast and been absorbed in some of the ancient cultures. He had come to Iquitos some days before, landing on earth and grass strips all the way from Trujillo in a thirty-year-old D.C.3. Like I, he had come with the intention of going up the Amazon. He had come with no idea what facilities existed to make the trip, whether it was safe or likely to be a worthwhile experience. Unfortunately, he had fallen ill with a fever and spent two days in bed. He still looked pale and listless. Later, when I saw him eating food prepared by Indians in the jungle, and drinking liquids fermented by the saliva of jungle children, I began to wonder how many days a week he had free from stomach trouble when he was abroad. I saw him tackle several dishes which looked almost obscene. He ate them with the expression of a man playing Russian roulette with a revolver he did not trust.

" I've got over my little illness," he said with a wan smile, " and I want to get off up the Amazon."

He told me that he had heard I wanted to go up the Amazon, too, and suggested we should join forces.

" It would be far better for two to go together," he said. " I'm fixed to leave here tomorrow morning. Why not let us join forces?"

There was Anglo-American co-operation in most fields these days, I told myself. I did not see why two people of Anglo-Saxon stock who spoke the same language and had so much in common should not do the journey together. We were both inveterate travellers who preferred to travel off the beaten track. We were both writers. We had both entered journalism as black and white artists. We both hoped to get some copy out of the experience though neither of us had come for that express purpose.

" Right," I said. " Let's discuss details."

We sat in the large flagged hall with its noisy punka and looked out on to the front. Unshaven, dirty old river men, who smelled like dogs and were more thirsty than hungry, patrolled the length of the windows, begging alms. Little, barefooted Indian boys tried to sell baby sloths, great handsome macaws, leoncites, marmoset, spider, saki, titi and squirrel monkeys, all of which Indians caught in the jungle. Or they tried to interest us in alligator skins or ocelot pelts. Brown actually bought an alligator skin.

We fixed a rendezvous for next morning. The boat he had hired seemed to me to be ridiculously small for a river given to such disastrous moods but I was determined to raise no objection. In for a penny, in for a pound. The craft would carry four. It had a 40 h.p. Evinrude outboard motor and sounded very much like one my Aunt Bertha uses on a large mill pond in Warwickshire. We were to be accompanied by a driver and a bearer, both young Indian-Spanish half breeds. These men would be able to lend us all kinds of equipment including 16-bore shot guns for when we went alligator hunting (this was included in the deal); snake boots, machetes (for cutting our way through the jungle undergrowth); torches, and a few other semi-necessities. They were going to arrange for us to stay near to Indians in the jungle the night before we penetrated deeper into the forests. I had only to pay half the cost of the trip and buy a quantity of tinned food. When I chose my provisions I evoked the emotions of war time days. I used to come from the Western desert with a mandate from my colleagues in the same unit to buy such luxuries as tinned salmon, tinned pears and peaches and tinned chicken.

We met punctually next morning, probably because the parrots had kept Brown and me awake most of the night. The Indian driver was a hard-bitten little know-all who had a ready answer for every question. He would have won a fortune in American quiz games on the television. The bearer was brash, noisy and given to singing Indian love lyrics at the top of his voice.

Together we crossed the road, broke through the balustrade, which was already falling into the Amazon, and slid down the sheer bank to where the boat was moored. The Amazon was in spate, so I thought. It carried past us, as if they were matchsticks, the limbs of giant trees of the forest. The river, as it happened, was merely dawdling. After a storm the river moved with the speed of an express train and carried away chunks of land from the banks as large as some islands on the Thames. I could well understand when I came face to face with the river that it carried a fifth of all the fresh water on earth, discharging it at the rate (not my calculation) of 3,400,000,000 gallons every minute into the Atlantic. I remembered seeing, as I flew into South America, the Amazon's silty brown stain 150 miles from the coast.

The mighty river was deserted except for a few old river boats tied up, and dug-out canoes and thatched, home-made water-buses in which squaws commuted between their turf-roofed huts and floating shops. The only big ship which made a scheduled sailing as far as Iquitos—and its arrival and departure caused a stir among the river folk—was a ship of the Booth Line, which came monthly with supplies and took on exports. Even today some provisions which were too heavy for air freight came from Lima through the Panama canal, down the Atlantic seaboard and then up the Amazon, to be taken aboard the Booth Line ship for Iquitos. Beer used to be brought that way, sometimes still is. The beer is bad enough. It travels badly!

The Amazon is slowly threatening Iquitos. The city fathers are aware of it and have held many futile discussions on how the angry river can be pacified. As our motor boat left its mooring below the hotel I could see how the tide was eating into the bank, washing away chunks of earth as big as golf tees. The driver took us round by Belen, the native quarter of Iquitos, where the Indians and half castes live mainly in boats, on river-side hovels built on stilts over the water or on the steep banks, one ramshackle building above the other. Belem was packed with ill-clad, or half clad people, with scraggy mongrel dogs, scrawny fowl and little black pigs. Overhead flew what looked like a death patrol by hundreds of great black vultures who seemed to know the high mortality rate and to be eternally on the lookout for a new corpse. The government admitted that the local water was polluted and that it was the cause of much illness. Many of the inhabitants were pale and thin, infested with intestinal parasites, three kinds of dreaded worms, or they were victims of the town's great curse, anaemia.

A few of the children waved to us, not vigorously with wide smiles as children elsewhere, but listlessly and with scarcely a show of happiness on their faces. The shade temperature was 94 degrees with high humidity but it was not the heat that had drained them of all energy.

As our boat ploughed through the river at some 30 m.p.h., leaving behind the last straggling suburbs of Iquitos and the last wretched water bus, the sounds of the jungle began to manifest themselves over the chugging of the engine. From the distant tree-flanked banks, and from a long island completely covered

F

with undergrowth, I could hear the well-known sounds of the jungle, the clicks, chirps, croaks and bleats. The background to all this was a low, perpetual throbbing as of a powerful motor that was idling. It was the mysterious public heartbeat of nature in the raw, a beat that was regular and rhythmical and yet had no visible origin.

The Amazon was deserted. Not even a canoe appeared. Our bearer pointed out to us a bend in the river where a 21-feet-long anaconda snake of the boa-constrictor family had been caught the week before and he took fiendish delight in describing it in monstrous detail and in pointing out the exact spot (over which we passed) where it was seen. Such snakes are of two kinds. One lives in the water, the other on land. Both sting a victim insensible and then squeeze him to death. The bearer lived for the river and knew it well. He told us stories about the animals in Amazonia, lapers, ocelot, jaguar, trigrillo, alligators, armadillos, opossum, ant-eaters, puma, and peccaries and described endearing characteristics of each. He told how some animals are caught for sale. Monkeys fall easiest into the trap. They love bananas and the Indians, knowing the animals visit their huts when they are away, leave bowls of ripe bananas mixed with *masato,* a strong, home-brewed intoxicant. When the Indians return they find the monkeys either fast asleep or rolling about drunk and have little trouble in fastening them up in some room to await a dealer, who buys them. Civilization was receding fast. The line between order and savagery was fast approaching. Now there was no sign of the works of man, only the wild, always magnified products of nature.

The noises of the jungle became more insistent, louder, more sinister, as if the deep undergrowth and the bushy trees which crowd right down to the banks were infested with all kinds of beasts watching us go by. Now and then there was a grunt, or a scream, or a monstrous chattering, or something fell plop into the steaming water to send out ever larger circles and to cause echoes to reverberate in the forest.

Millions of trees and billions of gallons of water later, our faces burnt red as beet, we climbed to the bank and went in Indian file, machetes swinging at anything that looked capable of life, through the thick undergrowth of the jungle. After a long walk we came upon a fifteen-year-old Indian girl and her two children, fat and podgy with black beady eyes who stared at us for a full minute and then ran away with the speed of a gazelle. Even Iquitos seemed a long way off after that. Each arduous step we made through the thickets seemed to put miles between us and civilization. I wondered if I would be able to sleep that night.

XXII

Night in the Jungle

DARK FELL like a blanket, enveloping us all. It was then that I felt isolated. It was then that even the worst B.B.C. television show would have been a boon. It was then that we longed for a lamp-lit street with the man in blue keeping his eye on the traffic-lights, as if some thief might run away with them. The contrast between the well lit, broad streets of Lima with their constant streams of traffic, the clamour, the street cries of vendors and this silent, yet throbbing, backwater was almost unnerving. The idling motor of savage nature got into full gear as night wore on. The Amazon became a noisy workshop, in which I swear I heard hammers on anvils, belts singing on pulley wheels, trolleys clattering along railway lines. Between all this pseudo-mechanical background noise there were animal shouts and screams, cries of agonizing pain and loud trumpeting that caused a physical shudder to run through the undergrowth.

Great insects flew around us, their wings incinerated in the flare lamps, so that we found ourselves walking on the squelching bodies of moths as big as sparrows, on huge praying mantis, on locusts, great shiny-bodied beetles that cracked like plastic when trodden on. Hundreds of fireflies streamed past us in the dark as if they were tracer bullets with phosphorescent heads. Some were flame red, others saffron yellow or field green. They flashed and blinked or burned brilliantly in the undergrowth and on the trees. Now and then, to left or right, there were strange sounds that had no counterpart in the life we had known before. I for one (maybe Brown too) felt sure creatures were watching our every move. And all the time there was the fine steely whine of the mosquito.

The bearer and the driver said very little, but busied themselves with the beds which were on wood platforms with grass-topped roofs, the sides wholly open to the jungle so that anyone could swing on one of the poles and lift himself into the 'bedroom'. It was easy to let the imagination run away with itself in such circumstances. Easy to imagine that the noise to one side or the other was that of a wild animal or that the moving object that hit one of the stilts on which the platform stood, causing it to quake, was a marauding Indian thief.

We ate our food and discussed what we should do. Someone, I think it was the tracker, suggested that we might go alligator hunting in the backwater, about twenty miles further on. Brown and I agreed gladly. Anything rather than suffer the gloomy boredom of that camp. We walked gingerly in the dark over the landing stage of felled trees, bound together with jungle bine stronger than cable, and got into the boat. The sky was studded with stars which reflected themselves in the broad river. The water was still except for the occasional plop plop of a white whale or some huge fish. The boat was pushed out from the side. As we glided powerless into the middle of the river a deep mystifying silence fell on us, something that belonged to some primeval world. It filled us with an inner peace. I chanced for a second, in the light of a torch, to see Brown's handsome face, pale and thin, and felt that he was enjoying every second of the adventure, even if he was wondering still again if he really ought to have eaten that last stew.

Now and then shoals of fish turned about in the water and we were left to conjecture whether or not they were the deadly piranha, the cannibals of the Amazon, found in plenty in this area, or merely an edible sardine of the kind we had eaten in Lima. The bearer, glad of the chance of a few gory details, told us they were probably piranha after all. He explained graphically how they attacked in shoals. They could strip man or beast to the skeleton in a matter of minutes with teeth that were like razors. I could never have fished in the Amazon for fear of what I might catch after hearing of the different kinds of creatures that lived in the water. The river contained 1,800 species of fish compared with the 120 in Europe. The names by which some were known were strange and terrifying.

Feeling cool for the first time as the night breeze met us we travelled in silence after that down the river until our eyes became accustomed to the dark, or rather to the half light from the star strewn heavens. The Southern Cross, and stars, so new and strange to those of us from the Northern Hemisphere, reflected themselves on the water to make the world magical. It seemed an age later, so absorbed was I in every twinkle, every sound and movement in the river and the enclosing jungle, that the engine of the boat faltered and was shut off.

Torches and guns were at the ready as we turned into the backwaters and the tributaries—the Amazon has 1,100 tributaries besides those which are uncharted—where the alligators are always found.

"It's just dark enough for hunting," said the bearer. "You can't see their red eyes in the moonlight."

The jungle noises were twice as loud and many times as sinister in the narrow creeks and backwaters as on the broad river after the motor had been switched off. We all stared breathlessly at the sides of the river. Wet, clammy creatures fell on to my head and into my lap as the boat glided without power under the branches of low-hanging trees into glistening lagoons. I must confess that I called out in alarm. I managed to catch one creature, cold and moist, struggling to get from between my legs as I sat tightly in the boat. I had the presence of mind to switch on my torch, fearing the creatures to be snakes, only to find green tree frogs squirming and wriggling to be off.

Time and again one, or another, or most likely all of us together, cried out as we sighted alligators on the bank or floating on the river. If we sighted the reptile while we were moving under power the engine would be shut off and we would glide, helped by oars, up to it. It did not dive as I expected. In nearly every one of some fourteen sightings the alligators remained there until we were nearly alongside. The reason for this was that the reptiles were asleep. Alligators cannot shut their eyes, only drop a veil over them, and this makes the otherwise yellow optics glow flame-red, visible from afar if in the shadows.

The bearer raised his gun to shoot on one occasion, but Brown protested. The animal was asleep, he complained. Besides, this was a white alligator, which generally ate fish, not a black one which ate human beings. It was agreed in conference in the noisy backwater, with night birds flying hither and thither, and animals unseen springing from branch to branch, that only black alligators would be shot.

So the night wore on and I found it far more fascinating and less uncomfortable than at the camp. The four torches frequently cut the dark into ribbons to awaken the day animals and birds to join in the nocturnal chorus. At times I thought the voice would shatter our eardrums. Then we were deflected by some stranger noise, a persistent rustling in the deep undergrowth, a sudden, almost overpowering smell of camphor, or some inexplicable bang.

"Yes," said my companion, "this is the world as it was at the beginning. I wouldn't have missed the experience for anything."

I found it impossible to sleep that night back at the camp. I felt as I could be expected to feel in the circumstances. The night journey up the river had eradicated my silly fears of intruding animals and Indians, but still something kept me awake. Brown was not within calling distance or I would have discovered that he too, could not sleep. I lay listening to the 'factory' noises of the jungle for some time before I realized that some of the sounds were distinctly human, wild and exhilarated but definitely human. Soon it became obvious to me that forest Indians had gathered a few hundred yards to the east of us.

I lay listening, sometimes thinking that the voices were advancing, sometimes that they were retreating, for at least an hour. At 2 a.m., desperate to know the cause, I put on my boots, gripped my torch and a machete, and went off to investigate. I found a large grass-topped hut on stilts about 500 yards away. It was packed to capacity with Indians who looked drunk with mysticism. In their midst were perhaps thirty candles, their spear-like flames dancing in the air. Though I did not know it then, it was the night when evil spirits return to haunt the living unless an all-night vigil is kept and the gods propitiated. To prepare for the occasion, the Indians stored up alcohol, made in a way which horrified me. They chewed roots, then spat them into a pot, where they fermented in time with the help of the human saliva to become pure spirit.

The Indians had come from over a wide area from clearings along the banks of the Amazon, all of them bringing candles which they had made from an animal fat, as well as items of food. The idea was that they should remain together, within sight of each other, to make sure that they were not spirited away in the night. They imbibed raw alcohol to give them Dutch courage. Now and then they broke into a chant with traditional songs which were supposed to propitiate the spirits.

I stood behind a tree for an hour and watched and listened

until an Indian girl, shy and unsmiling and nearly naked, began to
perform a strange ballet to the accompaniment of the clapping
of hands, wolf whistles and a low throbbing sound as if from a
muffled tom tom. I did not move until a huge fat Indian climbed
down from the platform. Then, fearful of being found intruding
on their rites, I hurried back to bed. I was still unable to sleep.
The Indians were obviously drinking themselves into a drunken
stupor. Their cries became more shrill.

XXIII

Untamed Tribes

NEXT AFTERNOON we came across a tribe of nearly naked Indians who hunt animals and birds for their food with the blowpipe, who fish with spears and nets made of forest bine and who pick their vegetables from bushes, plants and trees in the jungle. They lived in half a dozen large structures, platforms on stilts made with logs and trunks of trees and roofed with grass turf. They slept in hammocks, also woven out of bine and covered with broad, tough leaves. There was no furniture, only rush-matting on the floor. From the roof hung dried leaves, used for medicinal purposes, a few weapons and skins. Beneath the platform were logs for the open furnace, on which the community cooked, some dried fish and meat and bottles containing home-made alcoholic drinks, and sap from trees used for different purposes.

The bearer contacted the chief first for he could speak Quechua and several other Indian languages and dialects, and after a while he called to us. We were greeted by the ancient medicine man who wore a ' loin cloth ' made of reeds. Substantive dyes, made out of forest vegetation, stained his chest. Within a few moments we were surrounded by the entire community, apart from half a dozen men out collecting roots. The women were all breast naked and not even the young girls, who were prettier than I expected, showed any signs of shyness when they came up to us. If nearly all the tribe was present then there was a disproportionate number of babies and children. Each woman and girl, even those who seemed no more than fourteen, nursed a naked baby, and many children who could walk stared at us in wonder. We were greeted by music from bamboo pipes which the men had made but the girls would not dance though we asked them. Male and female were barefooted and wore only a narrow covering over their loins.

F*

I had the feeling that these hastily improvised garments had been put on as a concession to the prejudices of the white man and that normally they went about completely naked.

The journey from the camp had been a delightful experience. We had come along one of the prettiest stretches of the Upper Amazon, where there were dense forests interspersed with deep undergrowth and no signs of anyone having disturbed it. There were no animal tracks down to the water's edge, not to speak of paths made by human beings. Many of the trees were rare, nearly extinct, and I counted scores of varieties which I, as a member of the national council of Men of the Trees, had never seen. They were covered with blossom, sometimes red, sometimes yellow and, most often, shades of blue. As if nature compensated them, the trees which did not blossom were festooned with a wide variety of orchids which seemed to grow out of their trunks, sometimes near the head of the trees, but often from branches. Some orchids are not root plants as we know them but air spores which float on the wind to rest where nature designs. There were thousands of this beautiful, delicate flower hanging from trees each side of the river as if the aisles had been specially decorated to greet some distinguished visitor. Some of the spores had fallen on branches broken off trees in storms, or on to the fallen limbs of giants half submerged in the water, and the orchids grew on them. Flocks of butterflies, hundreds at a time, crossed the Amazon at a height of about ten feet above the water. Sometimes they were all flame coloured, or gold, or royal blue and they were reflected in the water. Each butterfly was large as a man's hands, placed side by side to represent the wings, with thumbs crossed in the middle, and the area of the water stained was, therefore, considerable. Now and then the motor was shut off and we glided into shallow backwaters as we had done lower down the river during the alligator hunt. We were shown in the water shoals of rare tropical fish of every colour imaginable such as one sees normally in an aquarium. There were pygmy catfish, covered with black dots; tetra with snout and forehead blood red as if they had been in a fight, beacon fish with head and tail lights, oblique fish, translucent fish and flying characin. In one lagoon I saw fish which were gold, with dark violet belly stripes, silver fish with green dorsal fins and bright red spots; orange fish sprinkled on the spinous parts with purple stripes; and chocolate-coloured fish edged with orange and with blue dots on the undersides.

As birds flew from one side of the river to the other they always occasioned cries of admiration from Brown or myself. They were large and of brilliant colours and emitted striking cries. Overhead betimes flew flocks of parrots. The journey was like watching a film in Technicolor, but with exciting scents and sounds thrown in for realism and, at times, sights so exciting that Brown and I nearly capsized the boat in our efforts to register the incredible creature involved on film. The river overwhelmed us with its sheer extravagance in every way, in the immensity of space, the implied immensity of time, in the superabundance of everything, the over-exuberant vitality of life, the sharp tonal and oral qualities and the clarity with which we could see details of everything in the brilliant light, even along tremendous lengths of the river.

The bearer said the Amazon regions were richer in plant life than any other part of the world. Orland Emile White, the agricultural botanist, says there are few places on the earth's surface where the struggle for existence appears so intense as along the Amazon. Plants literally swarm at several levels. The main feature is the forest and vast expanses of green-crowned columns spread on and on, out and out from a front of some two hundred miles until they seem to occupy the continent to the snow-capped Andes from the swampy tide water mangrove thickets at sea level to the bush country near the tree limit on mountains up to 12,000 feet. The forests are a promiscuous mixture of trees of numerous types, scores of species and a few individual types of each at a time. Their bushy green crowns all but conceal the sky. There are laurels, palms, myrtles, acacias, cedrelas, bignonias, cecropias, rosewoods, bombacaceas, rubber trees and purple hearts, to mention only a selection. In all there were 117 different woods, even in those parts accessible to officials. There were cow trees, silk cotton trees, umbrella trees, and the cream nut, and garlic trees and dozens of trees which bore fruit we knew and did not know. There were trees visited daily in season by the Indians for medicine and food, among them the quinine, coca, cassava (this provides tapioca) sarsaparilla, guava and tonks bean tree.

Like most Englishmen I love flowers, and though I prefer to see them growing wild, or in gardens, I have had great joy seeing the wonderful displays at Shrewsbury flower show, in my own county. I carried in my mind some of the more spectacular displays I had seen there, until I went to the Amazon. The natural flower shows I saw in the Upper Amazon eclipsed all that I had seen before, and there only Nature was the gardener and the landscape artist.

At times there were prodigious displays of red, pink, yellow, and white flowers, to which I could give no names, but only recall vaguely of what they reminded me. Their stalks were tall and strong and their petals fleshy. I identified the splotched pansy, begonias of several types, greenhouse latana, red and white heliconias, passion flowers, brilliant red calliandias and flowering cacti.

There were signs that Indians had lived in some parts, unless such vegetables as the potato, tomato and a type of onion grew wild. There were great ferns, scores of strong-smelling herbs, all of which had Indian names allusive to the complaints which they were supposed to cure when taken internally or applied externally.

Through the bearer I explained all this to the Indian chief and added that I had never seen such wonderful displays of trees, plants and flowers in my life.

" Many trees here," he said, " that white man wants because they make him rich but the Indians, not of my tribe but of others, they say ' no '. The trees belong to Indian, not white man. They grow fruit for us, or they give us sap which cures many illnesses. If the trees are cut down we lose our food, perhaps our vegetables, and also the birds and the animals which give us meat. We all very happy here, yes, there are some tribes which are at war, but that does not trouble us, and we want to stay happy. My friend here [nodding to the bearer] he told me just now that all is not so happy in the big white world from which you came, that there is war and misery because people are never satisfied and always want that which the other has. Here, we have nothing but what nature gives us, so there is no need for us to fight each other to get it. It all belongs to every one of us, to me and . . . [he looked around] and to that child which is not very well today."

I asked him if he had seen certain white explorers pass that way earlier that year. The Indian had been asked the question before. He believed both were dead, not killed by the Indians, though there were many savages. Only a few months before a group of white Peruvians making a recce had been attacked, three of them killed, six wounded.

I learned of white men who had sought sanctuary in the jungle, and left the civilized world for ever. Some had found what they wanted, peace and isolation from a world divided against itself, a world which was either at war or preparing and talking about the next war. Some had become ' renegades ', and led Indian tribes to attack white men by telling the Indians they would lose the best wood in the forests and be made to work hard for little as in the rubber boom days when 30,000 died in near slavery. It was also thought that criminals who had escaped from their own country to avoid punishment lived primitive lives as ' white chiefs ' of tribes. Some people swore that Nazis who had fled first from Europe to Paraguay or Brazil to avoid arrest as war criminals had crossed secretly to Peru. It was said that life in Paraguay had become impossible for them since self-appointed Jewish agents from Israel were trying to abduct them. One white man was said to have a hundred wives or concubines and to have bred his own servants, or labourers. He was said to be living in the depths of the jungle like an uncrowned king with his own government, his own troops and his own self-established economy.

I was taken over the living quarters where I saw primitive counterparts of modern kitchen utensils, things seen elsewhere in museums. I saw charms and omens in the shape of dried animal parts. I was told of the many roots and shoots found in the jungle and used as vegetables. The heart of the palm was a delicacy. Of the world's 23,000 plant species 20,000 had already been found in the Amazonian Basin. Food included wild turkey, quail, Pavas, duck, several types of monkey, geese, macaws, paca, capybara, parrots, toucan as well as wild animals. I was glad to hear they did not eat the majestic white heron, called the bride of the jungle, which was a delight to see. When a flock flew into a tree it seemed suddenly to burst into bloom and only then the orchids faded into insignificance.

The witch doctor told me how he treated the many minor complaints to which the Indians were heir. His tribe had escaped leprosy, which was common, yellow fever, and many other grave diseases. Malaria was rife, " but they had a cure." He could go to various trees, take sap from the trunks, and use it as antidotes to snake bites as ' cures ' for enteritis (though he did not call it by that name). There were about eighty different herbs he used, raw or boiled, internally or externally to meet recurring symptom complexes. If he was wrong the patient died and the death was attributed to evil spirits. If he recovered there was a celebration with liberal doses of a milky sap from another tree that seemed to be the jungle distillery.

The Indians knew little or nothing about the outside world and the wonders of the twentieth century, and cared less. They were uncounted and accountable to no one. They did not handle money but carried on trade with other Indians. Their needs were of the simplest and so were their troubles, although the incidence of ill health and early death was very high.

" We are happy," a sixteen-year-old girl told me, through the interpreter. " There is everything here we need, all the fish in the river, the fowl in the skies, the meat in the forest. We make our own boats and visit other tribes and make friends with them. We collect our own wood for making fires on which to cook. We do not need money for anything, nor do we need to work for anyone. We are happy and independent and we want to remain like that."

The sun blazed down unmercifully and Brown and I sweated the slightest effort we made. The Indians, used to the heat, as to the primitive conditions, were cool and happy in their loin cloths. They did not require clothes or footwear excepting what they made for themselves. They knew nothing about radio or television. When I said the air was full of voices, even of music, they thought, or pretended to think, that I was referring to the spirits in which they believed.

Who were the savages? I asked myself. The forest Indians or the people who made atomic bombs? The only purpose of the bombs could be to obliterate all life on earth.

Day after day I heard references from the two Peruvian Indians who accompanied us, to a battle in the Amazonian jungle. Finally, my curiosity getting the better of me, I sought details. There was not one battle, I learned, but several. There had been three serious skirmishes earlier in the year, but this was nothing un-usual. There had been many fights between the forest Indians and white prospectors. Three Peruvian prospectors had been killed in the latest conflict. Some twenty Indians, naked, with shoulder-long lank black hair, had died, or so it was said. The wounded men were rescued by an air rescue helicopter of the U.S. Air Force which was flown in for the purpose in a C-130 transport plane from Panama to Iquitos where it was unloaded for the jungle search. The rest of the party, numbering some fifty men, might have been slaughtered by pursuing Indians. They were rescued because a motor launch of British manufacture sold to the Peru-vian Navy was able to travel up a so-called unnavigable river and take the party on board. The British vessel, the 159-feet-long

Maranon, constructed by the Southampton firm of Thorneycroft, was the hero of the incident.

" They're wonderful boats," Sir Robert Marett, British Ambassador to Peru, told me when we discussed the incident in Lima. " They can go almost anywhere. I was glad to learn that one of the boats played such an important part in this rescue."

The first attack happened less than a hundred miles as the crow flies from the area in which Brown and I went out hunting alligators—that is between the Amazon at its broadest, where it bulges out like a python after a huge meal, and the Yavari River. There are several slightly different versions of what led up to the attack but it seems certain that the party of Peruvians, accompanied by Peruvian soldiers, had gone from Requena, an army guard post, with ten guards, through the jungle over the Tatina River and Galvez tributaries of the Amazon to see if it were possible to build a linking road. They were attacked by Mayoruna Indians without much warning. They were at a disadvantage because they did not know the whereabouts of the paths that led up to the point of attack.

Like every other party in the jungle the Peruvians had posted guards just before they retired for the night. They had also taken several other precautions for it was well known that forest Indians in the neighbourhood were hostile. The three Peruvians went off later than their companions to wash billy cans in the river only to fall into an ambush which had obviously been laid with care. It was clear to the Peruvians left behind in the camp that the Indians had been waiting for a small group to leave the rest. The Indians had been watching the party the whole of the time from the upper branches of leafy trees and from the deep undergrowth. One Peruvian was shot in the eye and died. The other two escaped, but the whole party was severely shaken up. The Indians withdrew for a while, and the party tried to get some rest, relying on their augmented guard. It was not long before sentries began to hear the cry of night birds. One of them, an amateur naturalist, noticed that some of the cries were not those of nocturnal birds, but strange, almost eerie cries made up by a mimic. Without making a sound he crept to where his mates were sleeping and gave the alarm. They were able to rise and be ready in case of attack without arousing suspicion.

" The attacks were uncanny," I was told. " The Indians made not a sound. They were like ghosts—sixty of them.

" Another was killed and a third was wounded in thirty-one places. Every organ of this man's body was perforated. He died later. The soldiers lost no time in getting into touch with the army guard post at Requena by wireless. They appealed at once for help to take out the wounded. They were told that every effort would be made to get a helicopter down into the jungle provided the besieged party made a landing ground and then, at an agreed time, signalled to the aircraft to indicate where it was. The party lost no time in making a clearing in the jungle while the guards kept a sharp lookout in case of another attack. The army post sent off a rescue party of forty armed men in a remarkably short space of time, which said a great deal for the efficiency of the Peruvian army. A colonel contacted the Air Force to ask if they could take out the wounded. The Air Force could not do the job. Alouette machines were needed. Contact was made with the U.S. Air Rescue Service at Panama, who were known to possess such helicopters. Unfortunately there was another set-back. The station had the helicopter all right but they had not the means of transporting it so great a distance to a point from which it could be used to fly into the jungle. The deputy station commander lost no time in finding for this purpose a Hercules C.130 to carry the helicopter to Iquitos for its flight to the jungle."

Meantime the Peruvians in the hot, humid wilderness, kept constant vigil with their arms. They heard many more bird calls which might have been real or imitation: heard screams, howls and thuds, of which the jungle is filled. They even heard sounds like those of Indians infiltrating into the bush beside the camp, as if lining up for an attack on the clearing. The Amazon had never been tamed, let alone conquered. There was not a single bridge or power station or reservoir along its entire length. The Indian tribes who lived in the depths of the rain forest were also untamed and unconquered and were determined never to be.

Days later a U.S. plane flew overhead, obviously seeing the concentration of Indians converging on the Peruvian camp, and opened up with all weapons at their disposal. The area was machine-gunned and peppered with anti-personnel bombs. The plane then dropped supplies and flew off. Exactly how many Indians were killed no one knew. The helicopter arrived later and landed. Without wasting a minute it took on the wounded and flew away again. There was no question of taking off the able-bodied men. Much later a forty-strong rescue party arrived after a trying journey from Requena. Plans were made for them all to start at once on the long trek to the Yavari River led by loyal Indians the party had brought with them. A radio message told them that the Peruvian Navy hoped to be able to take a vessel up the Yavari River to a compass-bearing given. They did not hold out much hope however for the river was said to be unnavigable. The launch, which was British-made, had the reputation of being able to operate in such waters.

The party rested only for brief periods and then again set off. Soon the loyal Indian trackers reported that hostile Indians were following them at no great distance, at times fanning out as if to begin another ambush. The party decided not to take up defensive positions but to get to the river as quickly as possible. As the men struggled on, machetes swinging, Peruvian Navy personnel tried to navigate the Yavari River with its silt beds and sandbars and its hundreds of fallen trees. The *Maronon*, with a draft of only four-foot-something, negotiated one obstacle after another but all the time the water became more treacherous, less deep. Progress had been so far only possible because the vessel had the bow and stern of a speedboat.

Their flesh and clothes torn by thorns, the Peruvians arrived at the riverside with the hostile tribesmen hard on their heels. They could not see the *Maronon* at the rendezvous arranged by wireless. They used the wireless time and time again without raising the boat party and all the while they heard the bird cries which the Indians used as signals. It seemed hours later before one of the wireless operators picked up a message from the *Maronon*: " We are nearby and will be coming down."

The *Maronon* arrived and the men crowded on to it.

XXIV

Thunderstorm

THERE ARE many things to fear up the Amazon, more even than one suspects. Pure water is the greatest personal problem, for that which is available near to Indian camps is infected with all kinds of germs and spores. It would probably be safer to drink out of the river far from where the Indians camp.

But it was actually the pure water, the rain from heaven, of which I was afraid. When rain falls in the upper Amazon it falls by the billion gallons, and to the accompaniment of terrifying thunder and lightning. The lightning fells the tallest trees, which roll into the river as it rushes to the Atlantic with the speed of an express train. From the start, despite that I had been warned about bad water, savage Indians and snakes, my greatest fear was a thunderstorm while on the Amazon. I had no wish to be thrown into water infested with lethal creatures. Even the tributaries which flow into the Amazon at the height of tropical rains create treacherous cross-currents and whirlpools and threaten to overturn a small craft.

The weather remained perfect, a little too perfect, perhaps. Our faces became red as beet, the skin peeling off them as off new potatoes. It was not until we were returning to Iquitos that the sky clouded suddenly and the 94 shade temperature dropped with sensational suddenness.

"We'll get back long before the storm," said Brown, who was always optimistic even when faced with a dish of questionable jungle food.

The 40 h.p. Evinrude engine had given us good service. I had been very glad that it had not broken down when, for instance, we were up some remote backwater of the Amazon at night. Then we would have had to wait until someone found us, probably days later. Now, however, the engine gave an ominous splutter, forty miles from Iquitos, on a part of the Amazon where there were no canoes or boats with outboard motors.

"Hello, trouble," said the driver, and he climbed to the back of the boat. We watched the ever-darkening sky as he tinkered with the innards and wondered what would happen if marooned with no protection from the storm that was obviously not far away.

At last he kicked the engine in the right places and we got going again, but not for long. The trouble was more serious than we thought. Again we floated helplessly with the tide while the driver made another inspection. This time all the kicking (and swearing), were of no use.

Anglo-American co-operation had gone well. Both Brown and I had said how well we had got on together. The secret may have been that we had enjoyed every moment of our stay up the Amazon and been interested in everything we had seen. We had not had to wait for each other in places which bored us or compromise when considering alternative routes. Now we just stared at each other in silence. I do not think we would have spoken very pleasantly if we had had something to say. We were both tired and hungry and in need of a bath and both of us feared the coming storm.

"No use," said the driver. "The water pump has broken. The silt of the river has acted like emery paper on it and worn it out."

"You mean it has packed up?" I asked. "That we are stranded?"

"Afraid so," was his unhelpful reply.

"Nice with the storm coming on," added the other Peruvian.

Brown said nothing but thought the more as he lifted his face to the heavens. The driver got back into his seat and paddled the boat to the side of a jungle island that was covered with thick undergrowth and forest trees.

The clouds were gathering like Indians for the attack and the river changed colour to a blue-black that looked like copying ink. There is a difference of thirty-seven feet between high and low level on this particular stretch of the Amazon and it was rising now.

Vast squadrons of black vultures, with evil, naked heads and necks, and wing spans of four feet, were artfully prescient of the coming storm. Their phenomenally sharp sight and smell would be alerted.

There were thousands of them strutting arrogantly like monarchs ashore. They swept down menacingly to fight each other with fearful-looking beaks over any scrap of offal. They haunted my mind as we waited, drifting, far more than did the savage Indians, the alligators, the boa constrictors or the fierce piranha fish around us.

I felt certain that we would all spend the night in the open on a jungle island as the rain lashed down and as the thunder and lightning kept us alert. Our sunburns pained us. The mosquito bites which had produced lumps all over our bodies began to itch. We were thirsty and there was no water to drink. I could not see how we could escape the ordeal of my dreaded Amazonian thunderstorm. It must have been my lucky day, in fact a lucky day for all of us. Suddenly we heard the poppety-pop of an outboard motor in the distance. An Indian waved to us.

After negotiation which at times seemed dismal, at times a little heated, it was agreed we should be taken off and returned to Iquitos and that the bearer should remain behind with the broken boat. The driver told him he could reach Iquitos, obtain a new water pump, and return before dark to rescue him, but judging from the look on his face, and the oaths he muttered under his breath, he did not believe it.

At Iquitos the driver could not obtain petrol, let alone a new water pump.

" He'll have to stay where he is for the night," he said.

The threatened storm broke but not until after we were safely in our rooms. Darkness enveloped us and rain fell in a deluge. Rain continued to fall with terrifying fury, making a noise like a corps of drums right through dinner and for the rest of the night. Standing at the window of my bedroom I saw, in the light of steel-blue flashes of lightning, accompanied by thunder which threatened to shatter the glass panes, the roaring Amazon, racing full speed through the jungle, carrying on its bosom huts and boats, trees and sizeable islands of turfed land with trees still upright on them. The river rose fast. There was terror at the waterside dwellings below my hotel.

I could not get the bearer out of my mind. Indians fear lightning when they are amid trees and he was surrounded by them wherever he went unless he paddled out in the crippled boat into the middle of the Amazon. Though I did not know it, Richard Brown was similarly concerned. Never in my life had I imagined that a storm could rage so furiously for so long.

It had seemed to me a pity people did not win the wild jungle terrain of the Amazon for civilization. In the forests there live some 80,000 Indians at a guess. They belonged to some fifty tribes and spoke different dialects. Most of them lived in aboriginal conditions, ignored by the outside world though their well-being is of great concern to Peru and Brazil.

The League of Nations, which had tried to help before the United Nations took over, once decided the Amazon basin could support nearly 100,000,000 people. The governments of countries through which the river flows had offered men land, with no rates, taxes or import duties on articles produced, or exported, for ten years, but few, as yet, have responded.

This vast area, larger by far than all Europe, could be brought into the orbit of civilization, if the nations acted together. Instead, those with the cash insist on getting to the moon.

CONCLUSION

ONE OF the greatest mysteries of all time is why Peru, and for that matter, America as a whole, remained unknown for so long to the West. The nations which were wealthy enough to embark on exploration, Spain and Portugal and England, would say that they could hardly discover the Americas in the normal way because they did not know they were there to discover. But in spite of this the Norsemen probably had knowledge of the New World some 500 years before Christopher Columbus. Columbus, who was financed by Queen Isabella of Spain, made his 'discovery' on 12th October, 1492, but there is ample proof that Leif Ericsson, in his eleventh-century voyages discovered the continent long before him. A mediaeval map showing a representation of America to the west of a well-drawn Greenland is said to document this pre-Columbian discovery of America. Count Eigel Knuth, the well known explorer, who carefully examined the map at Yale, said that he did not doubt that it was genuine. He added that reports of a Vinland, which newly discovered America was originally called, was known in the days of the Phoenicians and in the early Middle Ages. He thought the map might have been the conclusion of all the reports known on Vinland. The story of Leif Ericsson's discovery of America is told in Norse literature as the land of Vinland because grapes were grown there and it is believed by an increasing body of people. But whoever they were the early explorers found the New World only by accident as they sailed haphazardly with their inadequate equipment trying to find a new route to the East.

The explorers thought they had found India and that was why the people who then lived there were called Indians. American anthropologists have for generations held fast to the theory that all the ancestors of the aboriginal Americans developed their cultures without any help from the West. A minority believe the contrary was true, and declare that, in some strange way, peoples trekked huge distances over ice and snow to reach America from Asia. This is still without proof, although people point out the inexplicable cultural similarities on both sides of the Pacific, all of which could have derived from visits by Norsemen. There have, however, been similarities in other parts of the world without subsequent evidence of migrations. It is as difficult to prove that all the ancestors of the aboriginal American developed their cultures independently as it is to prove the contrary theory.

The biggest hurdle to the belief that the aboriginals developed their cultures without outside influence, or that they were indigenous to the American continent, are the people who declare that early man did not develop in the Americas but in Asia. This is based on the fact that no remains of anthropoid apes or of paleolithic man have been found there as in Europe and Asia. The nearest experts have approached to the later part of the second ice age's last glacial period is a discovery in a cave in Oregon said to be 9,000 years old. But what the experts do not take into account is that vast areas of South America which have not been explored may yet contain evidence which would upset global theories. The oldest evidence so far found has been in the Andes but no one has searched thoroughly the greatest depths of the jungles of the Amazon.

Waiting two days for a plane at a South American terminal I benefited by an intermittent lecture by a visiting anthropologist who seemed to have brought theories of his own with him on his first visit to Peru and with the intention of trying to prove them correct. He had a closed mind on the theory that the Indians of America, the Quechua in the highlands and the Aymara Indians of the tundra, had come from Asia through the Bering Straits in late glacial times. Primitive foot coverings discovered, which had been dated radio-carbonally shortly after the melting of the great ice cap in that area, did not influence him at all. He did not agree that there had been trans-Atlantic migrations affecting this area or even trans-Pacific migration, though he thought it most likely that Norsemen had discovered America centuries before Columbus and that they had probably made contact with aboriginal people on various parts of the coast.

The Andean culture began in the coastal province and passed

after long trials to the plateau to bring about a political and cultural coalition and form an Andean oecumenical empire. When North American archaeologists began serious investigation in Peru all the West learned were vague stories of the Incas and their fabulous empire. Stories of the massive monuments of the Indians of the High Plateau and their successors on the highlands soon came to support the evidence of the seventeenth-century Spanish writer Fernando Montesinos in his book written five generations after the Spanish spoilation of the Andean Empire. He presented the Incas as the beginning of Andean civilization. Archaeology soon rectified this and showed that the Incas were at the end of the disintegration of that Andean civilization. The fact is Peruvian archaeology is only in its infancy. Many great discoveries may still be made if the history of archaeology in other areas is any guide. Some important sites have not even been investigated and at least a dozen interesting sites have been found, vaguely uncovered and then left untouched because of lack of money and absence of deep public interest. So far one can suppose that there was maritime trade between the pre-Incas and Mexico at about the start of the Christian era and that there was probably earlier trans-Pacific trade contact with Japan.

It is not widely appreciated that, as I have outlined, two amazing civilizations emerged among the Indian tribes of America 4,000 years ago. Cultures developed and flourished quite separately from, as far as one can discover, any trans-Atlantic or trans-Pacific cultures. That these Indian tribes had a separate existence for a very long period within America cannot be denied. The civilizations appeared in the Andean highlands and on the arid coastal plains and in the tropical jungles of Central America, unknown to or unsuspected by other parts of the world. The beginning of the end came for the Indians in 1519 when Cortes and his Spanish adventurers landed in Mexico. They destroyed brutally the Aztec kingdom of Montezuma. They burned to the ground its capital, Tenochtitlan (Mexico City stands on its site). Nine millions of the population disappeared as a result of the Spanish Conquest as the Indian population of the new Spanish Empire fell by nine-tenths. The Aztecs were treated nearly as brutally as the Caribs who were annihilated soon after the Spaniards discovered them. The Maya and the Inca were treated nearly as badly. The fires of the Inquisition were lit in the name of Catholicism and uncountable Indians died in its flames. Then slave trade was introduced. Pizarro read of these inglorious exploits when he was a youth and he resolved to follow the example of Cortes, and see if he could also plunder the treasuries of South America. Pizarro heard of the fabulous empire of the Incas as he and his brigands rested at Panama. They immediately travelled by ship to the south searching for the Inca El Dorado. On the way they captured Indians and tortured them, as only Spaniards can, to make them tell of its location. Some Indians were forced to reveal that a great empire headed by a god-emperor called the Inca was to be found in Peru. His wealth was founded on gold, of which, they said, vast quantities were mined from the earth or obtained from the rivers.

For long Pizarro voyaged without sighting any place that resembled the landing place described to him. Then, late in 1527, while his men were gathered on an island in the Pacific, they received news brought by a larger and more modern ship, that the Spanish governor ordered them to return to Panama. The orders caused a division among the crew. Some were anxious to obey. Others, led by Pizarro, had been waiting only for a seaworthy ship to continue their search. Before the sun set the crew divided in two factions. Fourteen men, now known to have been the worst ruffians of the crew, volunteered to go with Pizarro to continue the search. It was these men who pioneered the way, inspired by the lust for gold, for an army of brigands who later, by cheating and by low cunning, treachery and murder overthrew an empire of several millions which had rapidly developed in importance over the previous century.

Because of vandalism, archaeologists and historians have had to work with patience for years to piece together the shattered story of the Incas and pre-Inca civilizations like the Toltecs and Olmecs, and further south, the Maya which preceded them. Archaeologists from many countries, including U.S.A., Germany and Japan, have searched patiently for evidence which they have pieced together to make a picture, still vague and incomplete, yet fascinating in its broad outlines. They discovered in ruins and graves in the arid deserts and stone remains in the tropical jungles enough to prove that pre-Columbian Americans were a great people of tremendous accomplishment. Their engineers had solved the greatest problem set by the geography of Peru, the distribution of domestic water, by using the principle of inverted siphon to carry it. One canal found in working order was eighty miles long.

Who is to say that even in this atomic age new evidence of the origin of man may not be found along with, even, new species of animals and plants? There are vast unexplored areas, forests and swamps and unscalable mountains in which we may expect still to find something new. There is such a possibility in the jungles of the Amazonian basin.

The age of major discoveries is thought to have passed with the last century, but new animals have been found recently, notably in and around Peru. These include the one-horned Pauxi cock (1939), the Andes wolf (1941), the large vicuna (1944) and the marsupial marauder (1943). The dwarf mara has also been discovered and a large sea snake is assumed to exist in the sea off the South American coast where, according to recent (and not so recent) reports, it was sighted by mariners. Other new discoveries include, at sea, the large scaly octopus though this species has yet to be recognized by science.

We might find the ruins of other, still more important ' lost cities ' under the thick undergrowth as well as new and not very mobile creatures in the Amazon jungles. These animals could be as sensational as the monstrous komodo lizard discovered in 1912, or the whitish-yellow guereza discovered in 1942 or the yellow-headed shrike discovered in 1934. Many other species are assumed to exist because of reports not yet confirmed and, therefore, not yet recognized by science—the waitoreke, the striped marsupial cat (seen in 1941, but not for long periods) the horned aurochs, and several others among them. At the moment some of them are the subject by scientists only of amused interest. Indians of the Amazonian jungles tell tales of encounters with mysterious creatures or declare that they have seen the tracks of huge animals in the swamps. Some who have said they have come face to face with creatures which conform to no known animal have brought witnesses to confirm their story. Scientists are very cautious about such reports, even if, as has happened, fur or feathers that belong to no known animal or bird species have been brought to their notice.

" We have only recently found, or rediscovered, animals thought to have died out," a naturalist told me. " We imagined they existed in museums only in fossil form or as stuffed creatures. One which caused great excitement was the latimeria which was rediscovered in 1939. Then, just think of the great lizards on the island of Narborough in the Galapagos group, terrible-looking reptiles that resemble the prehistoric saurians. Take it from me the Amazon could be an area of many discoveries."

It seemed to me to be a great pity that, while so much money is made available for experiments in Space, investigations into places on earth like the Amazon basin should be neglected for lack of funds. If in writing this book for people with no expert knowledge of archaeology or anthropology I have awakened popular interest in the remoter parts of the Andes and in talented Indians like Peta descended from the Incas then I shall have had my reward.

INDEX

A

Acapana (pyramid), 35
Aguas Calientes, 63
Alden Mason, J., 39
Altiplano (high plateau), 25, 26, 27, 31, 46
Alto, el, (La Paz airport), 26, 27
Amautas Indians, 109
Amazon, River 26, 137 ff.
Amazonia, 12
Amazon Basin, 11
America, 31, 36
Aran Islands, 105
Arequipa, 65
Argentine, 12, 13, 20
Arica, 13
Arica-La Paz railway, 13
Arteaga, Melchor, 101
Asia, 43, 59
Atacama Desert, 21
Atahuallpa, Inca, 36 ff.
Atlantis, 30
Aureli, Willy (Brazilian explorer), 126
Aymara Indians, 20
Aztecs, 45, 57

B

Babylon, 45
Balta, President, 59
Belaunde, President, 89
Bennett, W. C., 36, 38
Bingham, Hiram, 78 ff.
Bio-Bio, 13
Bolivar, Simon, 60

Bolivia, 12, 19, 21, 25, 28, 32, 37
Brazil, 13
Britain, 47
British Museum, 14
Buenos Aires, 28

C

Caesar, 74
Calachia, 120
Calca, 67
Cajamarca, 76
Cammel Laird, 48
Casas, Las, 85
Cave, Professor, A. J., 126
Chan, Chan, 65
Chavin, 43
Chile, 12, 13
Chincha Islands, 150
Chita, Plain of, 66
Cieza de Leon, Pedro de, 37
Collao, 39
Colombo, 11
Columbus, Christopher, 40
Cordillera Mountains, 83
Cortez, 74
Cuba, 100
Cusi, Titu, 120, 121
Cuzco (Inca capital), 17, 43, 59, 94 ff.
Cwn-Einion (Wales), 20
Cyprus, 31
Cyrene, 36

D

Diaz, Bermal, 135

Doyle, Conan, 82
Dyott, George, 125

E

Egypt, 34
Ekeko (Bolivian God), 33
El Dorado, 74
El Misti (mountain), 57
Elizabeth II, Queen, 47
Ericsson, Lief (explorer), 182
Espiritupampa, 118 *ff*.

F

Faucett, Elmer (pioneer flyer), 155
Fawcett, Colonel P. H., 124
Fawcett, J., 124
Franco, General, 77

G

Galera, 126
General Lagos (mountain), 21
Germany, 125
Godoy, Parez, 99
Gran Pajaten, El, 122, 123
Greece, 31, 57
Grivas, General, 98
Guaqui, 46

H

Hitler, Adolf, 99
Huancayo, 30
Huaylas, 21

I

Illamani, 26
Illampo, 26
Imhotep, 35
International Labour Office, 87, 88
Incas, 11, 13, 53
Inca nobles, 16
Iquitos, 130 *ff*.
Island of the Sun, 18

Isabella, Queen, 39
Israel, 71

K

Kansas City Star (newspaper), 138
Kenoco, 67
Kon Tiki expedition, 40
Krekovich, Kristian, 50
Kuelap, 122, 123
Ku Klux Klan, 34

L

La Paz, 18–25, 28, 33, 57
Lima, 11 *ff*.
Lucma, 112

M

Mache, 139
Machu Picchu, 39 *ff*.
Madeira, 26
Mallasilla, 26
Mama Ocllo, 50
Mancay, 67
Manco Capac, Inca, 43, 51, 63
Manco II, Inca, 11, 78, 119
Marett, Sir Robert, 175
Megalithic empire, 30
Meiggs, Henry, 48
Mendreta, R. R. M., 30
Menphis, 35
Mixtec, 78
Mohica, 45
Molloy, Father, 48
Morro headland, 13
Mu, 30

N

Napoleon I, Emperor, 70
Napo River, 130
Nazca, 45
New York, 38
Nino, El, 153
Nustas, 49